Eustace Clare Grenville Murray

Russians of Today

Eustace Clare Grenville Murray

Russians of Today

ISBN/EAN: 9783337168872

Printed in Europe, USA, Canada, Australia, Japan

Cover: Foto ©ninafisch / pixelio.de

More available books at **www.hansebooks.com**

THE

RUSSIANS OF TO-DAY

BY THE AUTHOR OF

'THE MEMBER FOR PARIS' &c.

'Vis consili expers mole ruit sua'—HORACE

LONDON

SMITH, ELDER, & CO., 15 WATERLOO PLACE

1878

DEDICATED

TO

HIS GRACE THE DUKE OF SUTHERLAND, K.G.

AS A TOKEN OF HIGH ESTEEM AND ADMIRATION

FOR HIS COURAGE AND PATRIOTISM

CONTENTS.

CHAPTER   PAGE

INTRODUCTION ix

I. A SQUIRE AMONG MANY 1

II. AN EMANCIPATED VILLAGE 10

III. A CO-OPERATIVE VILLAGE 19

IV. THE TEMPERANCE QUESTION 28

V. THROUGH THE STREETS 36

VI. THE BRISKATSTARTINE HUSSARS 46

VII. A VICTORIOUS GENERAL 56

VIII. A PROSPEROUS MERCHANT 65

IX. JUDICIAL BUSINESS 75

X. FORGED BANK-NOTES 84

XI. THE WHITE CLERGY 94

XII. THE DAIMONIKS OF EKATERINOSLAV . . . 102

XIII. A BOOKSELLER AND PUBLISHER 111

XIV. NEWSPAPERS AND REVIEWS 119

XV. MARRIAGE CUSTOMS 127

XVI. MONKS AND NUNS 136

XVII. SOCIETY 145

XVIII. THE GOVERNMENT OF POLAND . . . 153

XIX. ORDERS OF KNIGHTHOOD 162

XX. TRAVELLING 170

XXI. THE CZAR 178

Contents.

CHAPTER		PAGE
XXII.	THE CHANCELLOR GORTSCHAKOFF	188
XXIII.	THE CONQUESTS IN TURKESTAN	196
XXIV.	THE TRIBES IN TURKESTAN	204
XXV.	SIBERIA.—ON THE ROAD	214
XXVI.	SIBERIA : THE FREE COLONIES AND MINES	224
XXVII.	CHARITIES	233
XXVIII.	SCHOOLS	240
XXIX.	MILITARY ACADEMIES AND UNIVERSITIES	249
XXX.	POLITICAL AGENTS.—LADIES	257
XXXI.	POLITICAL AGENTS.—MEN	264
XXXII.	ENGLISH COLONISTS IN RUSSIA	272
XXXIII.	FRENCHMEN IN RUSSIA	280
XXXIV.	DIPLOMATISTS	289
XXXV.	THE FUTURE OF TO-DAY	297

INTRODUCTION.

EPITOME of the HISTORY of RUSSIA.

THE ANCIENTS only knew the South of Russia in Europe.

They divided it vaguely into Sarmatia and Scythia, and believed those regions to be inhabited by a number of independent tribes : the Roxolani, Iazyges, Agathyrses, Hippomolgi, Cimmerians, Taurians, Mœotians, and others. These hordes were said to live in tents, and the earliest reports of their customs describe them as drinking fermented milk mingled with horse's blood, which made them tipsy.

In the second century of the Roman empire, the Slavs, who were the primitive inhabitants of Northern Russia, invaded Sarmatia and Scythia and conquered all its tribes one by one. These Slavs, the oldest of European peoples, had Indian blood in their veins and were settled on the western shores of the Volga fifteen centuries before the Christian era. Their manners, were Oriental and their religion was a mixture of Brahminism and of the forest worship of the Germans. They were polygamous, fierce, and thievish.

In the 3rd century A.D. the Slavs were in their turn conquered by the Goths, who gradually extended their domination over all the hordes encamped between the Baltic and the Black Sea ; and founded between the Dnieper and the Niemen, the Volga and the Don a vast empire which comprised approximately the Russia in Europe of to-day.

This empire was overthrown in 376 A.D. by the Huns, and during the next four centuries the south of the Gothic country, as it was called, became the scene of constant wars. The Huns, the Alani, the Bulgarians, and Khazares successively reigned there and were expelled.

As yet no towns existed in the country, but towards the middle of the 6th century Kiew and Novgorod the Great were founded. The former as being the cradle city of the empire is known as Holy Kiew to this day. It was the place where Christianity was first preached in Russia and where Wladimir the Great was baptized in 988.

By this time the dynasty of Rurik, chief of the Varegi, had established themselves on the throne of the fallen Gothic empire.

Rurik subdued the Huns and Khazares and captured Novgorod in 862, and from this time the history of Russia (name derived from Rurik) properly begins. Rurik was a mighty conqueror and seems to have had governing abilities. His posterity rapidly consolidated their rule over the south of Russia and over Gallicia and settled their capital at Kiew. Under Wladimir I. they had become a powerful race and became the stronger for embracing Christianity, whose priests consecrated their authority to rule by divine right.

Under Jaroslav I. in 1020 they threatened Constantinople.

Then as now religious zeal was pleaded as the excuse for coveting the Byzantine city, and from that day to this the provinces of Turkey in Europe have tempted every sovereign who has reigned securely whether at Kiew, Moscow, or St. Petersburg.

Jaroslav was unable to conquer the Turks and under his successor Isiaslav (1054–78) feudal wars commenced and raged intermittently during the next four centuries. Christianity having organised Russia on the feudal system of Western Europe, Rurik's descendants scattered themselves as semi-independent princes at Novgorod, Polotsk, Smolensk, Tchernigov, Pereiaslav, Smoutatakan, Halicz, Tver, Vlodimierz,

Souzdal, and at Moscow founded by Dolgorouki I. in 1147. Every prince did homage to the Grand Prince who reigned at Kiew, but disputes about fiefs and appanages were continually arming the vassals against their sovereign or against one another.

Profiting by these civil wars the peoples of the East began invading Russia and several times were nearly bringing the empire to ruin. The Petchenegks and the Polovtses twice marched to Kiew and obliged the Grand Prince and his vassals to put aside their quarrels in order to make common cause against the enemy. After one of these invasions which had been victoriously repulsed ; a schism arose between Jourié (or George), Grand Prince of Kiew, and Dolgorouki I. prince of Moscow, who set up an independent throne. The separation lasted for eighty-six years, until in 1156 Isiaslav III. routed the Moscovites and restored the supremacy of the dynasty at Kiew.

At last in 1224 came the great Mongol invasion, which had about the same effect on Russia as the Norman Conquest had on England.

Touchi, the Mongolian chief, crossed the Volga with an army of 100,000 men and having conquered all the southern provinces of Russia instituted the empire of Kaptchak or the Golden Horde. His son Batou, reinforced by fresh myriads of Mongols, cap-

tured Kiew in 1240 and obliged Michael I. to fly to
Vladimir and thence to Moscow. Soon Podolia,
Volhynia, and Eastern Gallicia passed under the yoke,
and the Russians of the north, unable to keep up the
struggle, laid down their arms and submitted to be
Batou's vassals.

The Mongolian domination lasted 150 years, from
1240 to 1389.

The sovereignty of Kiew was abolished ; and
Jaroslav II. prince of Moscow received the title of
Grand Prince for himself and his descendants on con
dition of paying a yearly tribute to their conquerors.
Novgorod freed itself from the Moscovite connection
and set up as an independent republic under the protection of the Mongols. It looks odd to read of a
republic in Russia, but Novgorod became to all in-
tents a democratic commonwealth much more truly
republican than the so-called republics of Italy which
were oligarchies. The citizens had community of
goods ; and it is believed that socialist organization
of the modern 'Mirs' took its rise among them.
Anyhow Novgorod is proud to this day of having
once governed itself in freedom.

The rule of the Mongols in Russia came to an
end owing to their fratricidal wars with the Tartars.
The latter growing arrogant after their conquests in

India under Timour Beyg or Tamerlan, wearied the Mongols with their exactions, and forced them several times to call on their Moscovite vassals for assistance. A day came when the Russians got tired of shedding their blood for oppressors who burdened them with taxes and who in times of peace often pillaged their cities. In 1481 Ivan III. or the Great arose, like a Robert Bruce, vanquished both Mongols and Tartars, and drove them from the country. This done, he subdued Novgorod, Pskov, Biannia, Severia, annexed the Eastern portion of Siberia, and welded all his provinces into a strong empire of which he remained undisputed master.

Ivan III. was the first absolute sovereign of Russia, but he was satisfied with the title of Grand Prince. It was his grandson Ivan IV. who first assumed the title of Czar, derived from Cæsar, in 1533.

This Ivan IV., surnamed the Cruel, had to wage against his feudal princes the same sort of war as Louis XI. had waged against the French barons seventy years previously. He had inherited the throne when four years old, and during his long minority the boyards had had time to grow factious. Not content with subduing them, Ivan put to death as many as he could catch with the most refined tortures. He deluged his country with blood, and having restored obedience, burned the titles of nobility of all his boyards great and small, and decreed equality among his subjects. While doing all this he carried on successful wars against the Poles, Swedes and Tartars, conquered Kazan and Astrakan, and tried, though ineffectually, to seize upon Livonia. He has left a terrible name among the Russian aristocracy, but the common people are rather inclined to revere his memory, and a popular legend, similar to that of King Arthur in England, prophesies that he will return to earth at some period of national danger and free the mujicks from the oppression of their lords.

In 1598, fourteen years after Ivan's death, the dynasty of Rurik came to an end in the person of Fedor I., who was poisoned by Boris Godunow, his wife's brother, whom he had made prime minister. Boris Godunow seized upon the throne, but after a short and troublous reign was himself poisoned. He was succeeded by his son Fedor II.; but one Gregory Otrepiew, a monk, started up proclaiming himself to be Dmitri, or Demetrius (the son of Ivan IV.), whom Boris Godunow had murdered, and finding many partisans he deposed Fedor II. Soon afterwards he was dethroned by another pretender, who was in his turn routed by Vladislaw Vasa, a Pole.

It now looked as if Russia were going to perish,

for the Swedes and Poles had fallen upon it and threatened to march upon Moscow ; but taking alarm at the danger, the leading boyards met in the capital in the year 1613, and sinking their differences elected Michael Romanow to be their Czar.

Michael soon made peace with Sweden and Poland. By the treaty of Stolbova he yielded Ingria and Russian Carelia to Gustavus Adolphus ; and in 1618 signed a fourteen years' truce with the Poles, who had advanced within sight of Moscow, and surrendered to them Smolensk, Severia, and Tchernigov. A second treaty signed in 1634 confirmed the Poles in the possession of these provinces. But by this time Michael Romanow had fortified his country by judicious government ; and his two next successors, following his policy, became so strong that the Poles were at length beaten and had to give back Severia. The accession of Peter the Great in 1682 added to this prosperity and caused Russia to enter into an altogether new era of might.

Until Peter's reign Russia had been more of an Oriental than a European country. Peter set about Europeanising it and endowed it with a civilization according to his lights. He had to contend with the fierce opposition of a fanatical clergy and of the boyards : but he broke the power of the former by declaring himself to be spiritual head of the Church, and reduced the nobles to order by abrogating their privileges and abolishing their titles as Ivan IV. had done. As he was liked by the mujicks and possessed all the qualities of a master mind, he succeeded in everything he attempted. He founded St. Petersburg in the midst of a swamp, causing 60,000 houses to spring up there in ten years; he extended his empire to the Caspian and the Black Sea; saw the decline of Poland, and destroyed the military power of Sweden at Pultowa.

From this time Russia began to hold a foremost place in the councils of Europe.

Peter the Great died in 1725, and his immediate successors followed the lines he had laid down for Russia's guidance in his famous will, which has become, so to say, the charter of Russian Imperialism. They kept Russia mighty, without, however, adding much to its territory, and it remained for Catharine II. to take up the Great Czar's ideas and prosecute them in a spirit worthy of him.

This strong-minded princess, the Semiramis of the North as Voltaire called her, who reigned from 1762 to 1796, conquered Little Tartary, Lithuania, Courland, and the Caucasus, extended her empire to the furthest confines of Siberia; and in the two partitions of Poland which occurred in 1772 and 1795, obtained half of that ill-fated country. She also cast her eyes on Constantinople as Peter himself had done, but she did not live to realise the dream of her life, which was to transfer her capital to the shores of the Bosphorus.

Her weak, half-crazy son Paul only reigned long enough to join in the Coalition which Great Britain had raised against revolutionary France ; but he had a secret admiration for General Bonaparte, and was suspected of not acting fairly by the Coalition. Had he lived he would probably have made friends with Napoleon at the expense of England ; but his extravagant behaviour, bordering on madness, caused him to fall a victim to a palace conspiracy. He was murdered in 1801, and the crown passed to his son Alexander III., better known as Alexander I.

This Czar was also an admirer of Napoleon, but British policy kept him constantly in the anti-French Coalition except after the brief Peace of Tilsitt in 1807. Repeatedly beaten by Napoleon's armies, he yet contrived to add unceasingly to his dominions by the successive annexations of Finland, Eastern Bosnia, Georgia, and Bessarabia. In 1812 Napoleon's invasion of Russia having ended in a fearful rout, caused rather by the severity of the winter than by Russian generalship, Alexander cast in his lot with the Allies, and after two years' campaigning in Germany and France entered Paris in 1814, and had a chief hand in the restoration of Louis XVIII. to the French throne. The treaties of 1815 confirmed him in the possession of all the provinces he had annexed, and gave him about two thirds of Poland into the bargain.

Alexander I. dying in 1825 was succeeded by his brother Nicholas I., the hardest autocrat whom Russia had known since the time of Ivan IV.

It was Nicholas I.'s main object to prevent the Liberal ideas propagated by the French Revolution from spreading into Russia. He inaugurated a system of despotism which allowed no vent for public opinion and which bowed a huge nation of 70 millions of souls helplessly under his will and that of his creatures. It is computed that during his thirty-one years' reign not less than two millions of persons were transported to Siberia for alleged political offences.

In foreign affairs his policy was directed mainly against the Turks. He had made it the ambition of his life to conquer Constantinople.

He began in 1827 by fomenting the cry for the independence of Greece, and having drawn Great Britain and France into a league against the Turks, had the gratification of bringing about the naval battle of Navarino.

The Greek kingdom having been set up, England perceived a little too late that she had been drawn into a trap. Nicholas, proclaiming the Holy War of the Christian against the Infidel, prepared to cross the Balkans and march upon Constantinople. An injunction from the great Powers under the leadership of England stopped him just in time. But Turkey had already suffered immensely from this Holy War. Besides losing Greece, her sovereignty over Servia, Wallachia, and Moldavia was virtually broken. The treaty of Unkiar-Skelessi, signed in 1833, ratified these spoliations, and by hopelessly weakening the Ottoman empire paved the way for the Crimean War.

Nicholas calculated that Great Britain and France, who had been enemies for so many centuries, would never form a fast alliance for the defence of Turkey, and it was this mistake which impelled him to send his armies across the Pruth in 1854. The answer to this aggression was a declaration of war from the Allies, who were intent not on upholding Turkey but on maintaining the balance of power. The defeats of Alma and Inkermann proved too much for the ambitious Czar. He saw his prestige gone, his great dream laid in ruins, and it is suspected that he committed suicide. Anyhow he died broken-hearted.

Such is the summary of the history of Russia up to the time of Alexander II.'s accession. The principal events of the reign of the present Czar will be found alluded to and explained in the following chapters.

THE
RUSSIANS OF TO-DAY.

CHAPTER I.

A SQUIRE AMONG MANY.

OUR scene lies near the province of Kherson, in a dilapidated country mansion, built during the time when the refugee Duc de Richelieu was requiting Russian hospitality by converting Odessa into a flourishing city.

The *kniaz*—or Prince, as we indiscriminately translate that title in English—who reared the mansion was a noble of the third degree, who, reckoning his riches by 'souls,' as the custom was until sixteen years ago, boasted some 20,000 serfs. He was doubtless a friend of the French duke's, and tried to give his residence the look of those semi-castellated châteaux which are still pretty common in the midlands of France. He erected the

B

two gabled turrets and the lofty dovecot which on French ground betokened seignorial rights ; he did not forget the windmill, where his affectionate slaves were to have their corn ground for a yearly fee to his miller ; and he set up a granite pedestal, which still moulders in the centre of the entrance-yard, and marks the spot where the enlightened nobleman must have contemplated putting his own statue as a fit completion of the work which his architect had done for him.

But, like many other things begun in Russia under the impulse of a temporary enthusiasm for progress, Prince Wiskoff's country house was never finished, though a goodly number of plate mirrors were hung up in the grand drawing-room before the roof was fairly slated.   Prince Wiskoff, seeing these mirrors become mildewed, and finding himself rewarded with a touch of lumbago for his too great zeal in wishing to inhabit his mansion while the walls were still damp, took a dislike to the place and went off to St. Petersburg, vowing that men who devoted themselves to progress had always cause to repent of it.   The Prince's son never came near the crumbling new house at all.   The next Prince paid occasional visits to it, when he wanted some money and had a suspicion that his steward was robbing him. As for the present Prince, if we find him permanently located in a house with which rains, rats, and years have played such havoc, it is for the painful reason that his finances will not allow him to live elsewhere. Serge Wiskoff is forty years old, and spent the gay years of his youth in Paris. He married ten years ago, and, having left his wife's dower on M. Blanc's tables at Monaco, is now kopeckless, the father of five children, and a councillor of Court.

This does not mean that Prince Wiskoff ever goes to Court to impart his counsels; it simply signifies that he belongs to the seventh grade of the Tschinn, or organization of the nobility, and is supposed to hold a rank in the Civil Service equal to that of lieutenant-colonel in the army. Enrolment in the Civil Service was in his case a mere formality, intended to give him a position in that official hierarchy outside of which a Russian nobleman counts for nothing.

Prince Wiskoff began, at the age of twenty, as a college registrar, and, having never registered anything, was in due time promoted to a provincial secretaryship, whence, by the same process of doing nothing, he passed through a succession of high-sounding dignities, till he reached the present grade, which qualifies him to be appointed to higher steps, each one of which will entail a disbursement of fees to the Treasury. As these fees are pretty large, there is no chance of Prince Wiskoff being passed over when his turn of promotion arrives ; indeed, the promotion of Russian noblemen to functions which they never discharge seems to be an ingenious method for taxing them beyond their means now and then, while keeping them in good humour at the same time.

The Princess—or *barina*, as they call her on the estate—is so far from objecting to her husband's costly advancements, that she would cheerfully part with the few diamonds remaining to her if she could get him pushed forward at once to the ranks which would entitle her to be addressed as 'your high origin,' instead of ' your high nobility' as now.

We do not say there is anything of feminine jealousy in this, though the Runoffs, who own the neighbouring estate, are well known to be intriguers, who, by scraping together a little money to bribe clerks with, have become 'high origins' much before their time, and stick up their heads in an insufferable fashion at the triennial assemblages of the nobility in the starostate. There was even some fear a twelve-month ago that Alexis Runoff would be elected marshal of the nobility in his district, but the barina

Wiskoff was spared this crushing humiliation by one vote—that of old Count Stampoff, whom the Runoffs had made so happy with a champagne breakfast, before the meeting, that he voted for the right man by mistake.

Let no one be surprised that the barina should take such an interest in the triennial assemblage of nobles, for this is the solitary occasion in the course of three years when a Russian provincial nobleman finds anything of importance to do.

His important doings last about a couple of hours, and consist in the election of a marshal, nobiliary delegates or committeemen, inspectors of local police, schoolmasters, and petty justices. All the other business is abandoned to the committee-men, who may have a taste for such questions as claims for nobiliary inheritance, charges of dishonour-able conduct brought by one noble against another, land transfers, road-mending, rate-levying, and so forth. However, the session as a whole fills up some three days, and during that time all the princesses and countesses round about meet in the district town, make merry, and dispense hospitality. The barina Wiskoff invites friends to stay a week at her palace, and orders a slaughter of lean calves and pigs in their honour.

Out of the 650,000 hereditary nobles wherewith
Russia is blessed—not counting the 380,000 who are
not hereditary—many thousands stand in Prince
Wiskoff's dignified position, of having spent all their
money and having nothing to do. It may be urged
in excuse for them, that it was because they had
nothing to do that they spent their money ; for, if a
nobleman has no taste for garrison life or for employment in a Government office, what resources are open
to him in a country whose political system has been
devised expressly to check independent enterprise ?

Prince Wiskoff has thousands of good acres lying
waste because it would not pay him to sell them. There
are no decent roads near him, no canals or railways ;
and if he and some brother nobles were to club
together for an attempt to establish roads or railways,
the bribes they would have to administer to the
bureaucracy in order to get their plans licensed would
swallow up almost all the capital they could raise.

Ride through the provinces of Southern Russia,
and you come upon miles and miles of fruitful corn-
land, which might be converted into a granary for
Europe. Here you see acres of fine wheat rotting
uncropped, here herds of dust-coloured cattle wander-
ing about masterless and tainted with disease for want
of looking after ; farther on you come upon a luxuriant

plantation of tobacco, started as an experiment by some speculative boyard, who left it to its fate, because the tax he would have had to pay to the inland revenue for cutting the plants, and the trouble and cost he must have incurred in setting up a tobacco factory, would have left him no margin for profits.

Beetroot, maize, hops, vines might all be grown in Southern Russia; and it is not for want of foreign capital repeatedly tendered that the land remains a comparative wilderness, but the eternally grasping tschinn stands in the way of the foreign speculator, even more than of the native; and Serge Wiskoff, who is a tschinovnik himself in a small way, knows enough of the system not to ram his head against it by calling strangers to his aid.

One cannot wonder that the Prince should have found his estate a dreary place, and have lived in Paris so long as his money lasted, and if he ran through his fortune and his wife's more quickly than was proper, it must be remembered that he had been brought up to consider himself the everlasting owner of 20,000 slaves, and that men in such a case are not wont to haggle with their roubles.

The fact is, the emancipation laid the Prince on his back; for it was not accompanied by such a general reform as would have developed the capabilities of the country by striking off the official trammels that fetter it : in other words, the nobles, being stripped of the revenues their serfs yielded, were not free to make themselves incomes as country gentlemen do in other lands.

So poor Prince Wiskoff and his matronly barina yawn in their dilapidated mansion, whose walls are cracked and whose roof shakes at the least wind. They have a few gaunt, thin pigs grunting about their yards ; the village pope comes to give lessons in Greek to the children ; the district land-agent steps in now and then of an evening to drink vodki and play écarté with the Prince ; and the barina, when not troubled with household cares, lies on a sofa and reads French novels.

Yet Serge Wiskoff is an intelligent man, who, before he had grown rusty and crusty from poverty and idleness, was fitted for a better life than this ; and the barina herself is so conscious that she was fashioned to adorn the highest spheres of society that for years her one idea was whether money might not be begged, borrowed, or obtained by inheritance to enable her and her husband to go for another trip to Paris and enjoy themselves in hotels.

The present war naturally overturned these laudable schemes, for, like a good woman, the barina sent half her few diamonds and all her husband's spare cash to the Army Fund, firmly persuaded that while laying up treasure in heaven she was also putting out her gift to good worldly interest. So did the Prince think this. Like many another tschinovnik, he looked to the conquest of Turkey as certain to secure him a lucrative berth, and has for some months pictured himself as installed in Bulgaria and initiating that misused province into the benefits of the government system under which he has himself thriven.

CHAPTER II.

AN EMANCIPATED VILLAGE.

PRINCE WISKOFF'S tumble-down palace stands on the outskirts of a village more than a mile long, whose main street is twice as broad as Pall-Mall. The great size of this typical village comes of the fact that every hovel in it is fronted by a yard of an acre or two in extent, which serves no purpose but to accumulate dust in summer, and mud and slush during the three other seasons.

The idea of converting these plots of good ground into kitchen-gardens has never occurred to any of the peasantry; and Government, which meddles with so many things, has not thought it worth while to point out to them that if they planted potatoes, turnips, salads, and fruit-trees they might enjoy decent fare all the year round, and pick up some money into the bargain.

The Russian peasant grows white-headed cabbages and little else. These vegetables flourish in patches behind the hovels; when fermented they form the stock of the *tchi*, which is the soup of the lower orders, and of the *borsch* (mixture of cabbages and dried mushrooms) eaten by the middle classes. It is on cabbage alone, with an addition of maize porridge, that the peasantry may be said to feed; for eggs, bacon, milk, butter, cheese, and all the other edibles of country life in Western Europe are unknown in the village. Nor have the peasants the hale looks of Western rustics.

The women, flat faced, tow haired, with red-rimmed eyes and broad nostrils, prowl about in knee-boots and long sheepskin garments like the men. They are lazy, smileless, and silent, except when drunk on corn brandy, which makes them howl and romp. The men also require vodki to rouse them from the indolent moroseness which is their habitual mood, though they are active enough in rendering any service that may bring them a ten-kopeck piece.

Peep into the huts of these odd creatures, and you find a floor of hardened manure, a table, a couple of benches, a stove, and an iron statuette of the Virgin in a niche. There are no beds, chests of drawers, or anything to suggest the use of linen and the washing of the same. The stove-top is the favourite sleeping-place during cold weather; in the

hot months father, mother, and children curl themselves up like caterpillars, and lie down in corners.

One need not wait for night to find a whole
family thus sleeping. After the midday meal has
been eaten, the peasant will as often as not lie down
and snore away the whole afternoon, as if, next to
vodki, he knew of nothing on earth so good as idleness.

Why should the man work, since he has never yet
been taught that work is profitable?

We are passing through a village, whose inhabitants, before the emancipation, were all serfs of
Prince Wiskoff. The Prince's agent in those times
used to thrash them into industry in order that his
master might have money to gamble with and he
himself money to filch; but as the serf's condition
was never bettered by his hard labour—as, on the
contrary, the more he toiled the more was expected
of him—he naturally took a distaste for the practice
of exerting himself; so that when the emancipation
was decreed, he concluded that his working days were
over.

He has stuck to that idea ever since.

He would work for a fair wage if it were offered
him; he would even accept a hint about planting
those potatoes and turnips if he were furnished with

the seed and assured that he might eat the produce when it came up ; but he has a shrewd sort of notion that if he bettered his lot overmuch by labour he would draw upon himself the attentive eye of the taxgatherer. This exacting official, the exciseman, the land-agent from whom the cottage is rented, the peripatetic Jew from Odessa from whom money has been borrowed--all seem to be in a league to pocket the mujick's earnings ; and from what little remains when they have all had their share the parish priest begs the biggest half.

But the peasant gives willingly enough to the priest —or rather to the Church ; for priests individually are neither liked nor respected in Russia. In this miserable village, so filthy and poverty-stricken that the fierce, spare-ribbed dogs who gad about can scarce find a bone or bit of offal—in this place of dust, mud, and squalor—rises a church which would be deemed an ornament to any Western capital. Fair without, it glitters inside with splendid treasures bought in the holy city of Kiew. The altar is of marble, the candlesticks of silver, many of the images, crosses, and pictures are thickly encrusted with gold ; so are the vestments of the priest, the Communion-plate, and the font—this last being cut out of a solid block of malachite.

For ages the piety or superstition of Prince Wiskoff and his ancestors, of the land-agents, of the mujicks—of everyone, in short—has enriched this church with voluntary gifts. In old days a serf who obtained his freedom never failed to bring his votive offering, and if he went away to prosper as a merchant in one of the inland cities he would send offerings annually till his death, to the end that luck might not desert him; the Wiskoffs, also, whether they won at the gaming-tables or lost, always found money to pay for some new chalice or statue, and to this hour the peasants will club together every year to make some costly present the richness of which consoles them for their own poverty.

To the Russian peasant, indeed, the church is far more of a home than the hovel where he dwells. He enters it at all times, and may be found kneeling for hours opposite the shrine of his favourite saint, and gazing with ecstasy at the gorgeous things which fill his foggy mind with visions of Paradise. Perhaps he dreams of being himself clothed some day in gold brocade like the saint in question; anyhow, be he never so poor, drunken, and desperate, he would not steal so much as a pin from his church. Nor would a professional brigand dare to commit such sacrilege.

Sometimes in travelling over the windy steppes

you come across a gang of small-eyed, wiry little men, mounted upon yeo-necked galloways, with uncombed hair of rusty brown floating down their backs and ugly weapons stuck in their girdles ; and you know these men to be banditti, who would make no more fuss about robbing a Jew pedlar than about sticking a stray pig and roasting him for dinner. But let the Jew have consecrated ornaments in his pack, and they will piously sign themselves, leaving these things to his care, and purloining only his furs, knives, horn cups, pinchbeck trinkets, and such like, whereof, as we know, the saints take no account.

One day a pedlar being overtaken with a rather valuable cargo of profane jewellery got out of his scrape by flourishing in the faces of his would-be depredators the shin-bone of a holy martyr which he had purchased in the Kiew catacombs. The pious brigands only waited to see whether the Kiew mark (a dove and cross) was duly imprinted on the bone, and then scampered off, disgusted that such a precious article should be in the hands of an infidel, and yet not daring to rob him of it.

Look now and see a cloud of dust whirling up in the village road, and hear from the midst of it the wild 'yahoop' of a coachman. This is Prince Serge Wiskoff being driven to mass in his *paracladnoi*—a thing like a springless donkey-cart, drawn by three shaggy ponies, which gallop like the wind. The bearded driver, perched on a high seat, belabours his team without mercy, and yells because a noiseless progress would not befit the dignity of his master, least of all when going to divine service on a saint's day.

For this is not Sunday, only one of those frequent saints' days when what little work is done at other times is suspended and the entire population devote themselves to religion and vodki. The Prince is too well versed in French literature not to be a Voltairian, but he has prudence enough not to neglect the outward observances of his faith ; for if he did, the prestige which he still retains among his former serfs would vanish.

As it is the peasantry treat their old master with a fair show of slavishness. They no longer duck down on both knees when he alights among them at the church porch, as they would have done of yore ; but they bow with a profound humility, address him as 'little father,' and fawn upon him for gifts of money. Before the day is over he will be obliged to empty his purse among them and, having refilled it (with very small coin), to empty it again ; for although he can so ill afford to give, it suits him to play the magnificent, just as it suits the barina to be gracious and charitable to the women folks.

The Wiskoffs well know the peasantry nowadays have got imbued with some ideas which might prove very awkward in time of trouble to noble families who are unpopular. No newspapers penetrate among them, the village pope does not talk politics, the publican who keeps the brandy shop is a loyal, taciturn person, and yet here is not a peasant but grumbles that the Czar—their good father—would do a great deal for his people if the nobles would only let him.

He hears these things from the righteous pilgrims who pass through the village, begging their way from place to place as far as Kiew; he hears them from the Jew pedlars, who hate the Government, its Tschinn, and its nobles, with an intensity of hatred, and who, as they tramp about the country, scatter discontent broadcast; he hears them from soldiers returning, sullen and penniless, after fifteen years' service; from bands of howling fanatics belonging to some new-fangled sect, who start up in the village one day, shriek nonsense for a couple of hours, and then troop away, to be no more heard of; and he hears them again from emissaries of secret agrarian societies, who spread their treason with the greater ease as they can afford to bribe the police to let them alone.

The mujick has no wish to hurt the Czar, whom he worships as the fountain of all good ; but let the signal of revolt be given, and he will rise up, in the Czar's name, against the nobles and tax-collectors, and woe to those who will try to make him hear reason in those days when he will have taken up arms for one of those wild, unrealizable dreams such as can only dawn in the skulls of the ignorant and wretched !

CHAPTER III.

A CO-OPERATIVE VILLAGE.

How comes it that Prince Wiskoff, having many thousand acres of fertile land, can afford neither to till nor sell them, and remains poor ? How comes it that his peasants in the village we have visited are as idle as if they had a direct interest in being so ?

The peasants are idle because plots of ground are rented to them on short leases of a year, and they find no profit in improving these holdings since they have no security of tenure. If they brought up fine crops their rents would be raised and so would their taxes. Moreover, they are all, without exception, in debt either to usurers for advances made to buy tools or to their landlord himself for arrears of rent ; so that if they appeared to be earning money they would be asked for more than they had got, and their last state would be worse than the first.

As it is, they give the tax-collectors what they must and their landlord what they can, which is not a great deal ; the landlord, on his side, must be content to see them ruin his land by barbarous methods of cultivation sooner than turn them off and get nothing. It may be asked why he does not farm out his estate in large holdings and at long leases, but the difficulty is to find farmers. Men who have capital and experience enough to undertake a farm are scarce.

In places where the experiment has been successfully tried the landowners were themselves good agriculturists who resided upon their estates and kept a constant watch over the farmers, who else would have impoverished their soil and dragged them into costly lawsuits ; besides, both farmers and proprietors have to contend against this obstacle—that hired labourers cannot be got to fulfil their contracts. For fair wages the best among them, if well coaxed, will do a fair day's work, but, if they hear of better wages being paid elsewhere, they will troop off in a body, leaving the hay on the ground or the cut corn to take care of itself.

Others will hire themselves out to two masters, and after receiving a month's prepayment (which is customary) go away to drink and work for neither ; others, again, besotted by habitual intemperance, will at ordinary times scarcely work their wages' worth, and in mid-harvest will altogether decline touching scythe or rake for days together, because of church festivals which have to be kept sacred. The justices of the peace, who sometimes live dozens of miles from the aggrieved hirers, cannot easily be appealed to ; and when at hand do little towards enforcing a contract beyond sentencing the delinquent to three days' imprisonment—the complainant having generally to pay the costs of the process as well as the delinquent's carriage to prison.

All this brings agriculture to a standstill. Prince Wiskoff, like many others, is waiting for better times, without exactly seeing how they are to come under the present system of government. However, the vague hope that the extension of railways may put things straight in his children's time, if not in his own, prevents him from parting with his unremunerative property for the very low price which its sale would fetch him at present.

But let us leave this perplexed nobleman's village and proceed to another, which once formed part of the Wiskoff estate, but is now the property of a *Mir*, or peasant association.

The Mir system may be summed up in a few words : it has simply caused the peasant to exchange the domination of his old master for the more grinding tyranny of many masters. Nominally, he is the free

member of a co-operative agricultural society ; virtually, he is a bondsman tied to the soil he tills by a
load of debt, and unable to free himself or better his
condition by any amount of individual exertion. The
Mir village is as beggarly to look at as the other we
have seen, but there is this difference : that when you
have passed a mile's length of battered hovels and come
in sight of the usual beautiful church, with its inevitable sky-blue dome and gilt minarets, you suddenly
descry a row of quite handsome cottages, built of red
brick, with substantial doors and windows, and rather
resembling new Swiss villas.

These are the residences of the startchina (mayor)
and of the starostas (elders or aldermen) ; and their
prosperous state at once tells a story, for the Mir officials are not supposed to possess a kopeck more than
their fellow-commoners ; and if they do it is because
they peculate, and are furthermore influential enough
to get themselves re-elected over and over again that
they may go on peculating.

Here we see the startchina step out of his house—
a yellow-bearded, blue-eyed person, with a square
furred cap and a fine new sheepskin *touloupa*, girt at
the waist with a black silk sash. He is in deep conversation with a commercial traveller, from whom he
has been buying some agricultural machinery for his

Mir ; but he leaves him at once to welcome you, and
with soft winning Russian courtesy introduces you to
his house, where one of his sons, a boy in red-topped
boots and a white calico tunic, soon brings in some
capital tea, vodki, and cigarettes. The startchina does
not present his wife and daughters, for Russians of the
middle-class cling to the Oriental custom of secluding
their women ; but he comes and sits down with you
near the white-faced stove, and he has a most satisfactory account to give you of the village which he
governs.

At the emancipation, he says, the villagers (500
able-bodied men, not counting women and children)
entered into a bond to buy of Prince Wiskoff the land
which they occupied, for which they had been paying
him an obrok, or fief-rent, of 6,000 roubles. This sum,
at the legal rate of interest, 6 per cent., represented a
capital of 100,000 roubles, which the Mir proceeded to
borrow of the Government Land Bank. That bank,
however, in pursuance of its rules, would only lend
80,000 roubles—that is, four-fifths of the value of the
land—while taking a mortgage on the whole ; and the
loan was not advanced in money, but in bonds bearing
6 per cent. interest and payable in thirty-seven years.

Prince Wiskoff, being in need of cash, and only
able to convert his bonds at heavy discount, naturally

insisted that the Mir should make good this discount, as well as pay him the 20,000 roubles they had been unable to borrow by instalments extending over forty-nine years, with 6 per cent. on the unpaid sum. The terms of the bank were also 6 per cent. with forty-nine years of annual instalments ; so the Mir started into life with liabilities amounting to something like 12,000 roubles a year.

But another loan from usurers was soon needful to buy agricultural machinery ; and if we add to this the land taxes—the weight of which may be judged from the fact that the peasantry pay 195,000,000 roubles a year to the Treasury, as against 13,000,000 roubles paid by the landowners—it will be seen that this Mir works under rather depressing conditions. If the startchina thinks otherwise, the reason is very simple —it is he who, as mayor, negotiated all the loans ; who, with the elders, buys all that is wanted in the Mir for the common good (vodki included), and sells the produce of the community ; and it is he who, when a member of the Mir wants to go off and better himself as a workman or tradesman in towns, decides on what terms leave shall be granted him, and on what terms he shall buy himself out of the community, should he subsequently be able to do so.

Let us hope there are some mayors and elders who

rule their Mirs honestly ; but there is no public or
press to keep an eye on them, no officials charged to
audit their accounts ; and it must be recollected that
the more corrupt a municipal body are, so much the
greater is their chance of being re-elected, for with
the electors' own money they can buy all the votes
they want.

Now, under this system a peasant is much more a
slave than of old. He can marry at his pleasure, and
he is not liable to be cuffed or flogged (save illegally
as sometimes happens) ; these are the advantages he
has won ; but he is more heavily amerced than he used
to be, and nothing that he has is his own. If he
works too little his comrades abuse him ; if he works
his best he is no gainer, for all his earnings go into the
common stock, which somehow never yields a surplus.

There are years when the Mir cannot pay its
taxes. As the members are collectively responsible
to the tax-gatherer, it stands to reason that no one
of them cares to seem richer than the rest, lest his
superfluities should be seized for the common debt.
Thus, one will not think of breeding cattle unless all
the rest do, he will not dare to exhibit money he has
saved, and, in fact, what little he can lay by all goes
in vodki, which is the safest investment.

Of vodki there is always enough in the Mir, for it

is a means of government. It circulates by the pailful at election time ; it is plentiful on saints' days, when, if not drunk, the men might muster and grumble about their hardships ; it comes forth again in mysterious abundance whenever, from some cause or other, the mayor gets into evil odour and wants to regain his popularity.

Note that this mayor and his elders are never plagued by the tax-gatherer when taxes run short. The State official closes his eyes to the snugness of their homes ; he professes to find nothing seizable among their chattels, and always screws the deficit out of the peasants.

Some mujicks with more brains than others go away if they can find a chance of employment, and then, as we have said, it becomes a question between them and the mayor as to how much they shall pay. The least they can be charged is their full share towards the Mir's debt ; but if, growing rich, they want to liberate themselves for good, the mayor can assess a fancy value on their co-operation, and order them back if they refuse to pay it. The affair generally ends in a compromise. A sum is paid, of which the lion's share goes into the pockets of the startchina and elders, while the rest furnishes a good carouse for some or all of the other villagers.

Anything better calculated than all this to breed general idleness, wretchedness, and depravity can hardly be imagined ; but it also breeds this idea among the peasants—that they did not get a fair start after the emancipation, and ought to be exonerated from all their debts to the Land Bank and Prince Wiskoff.

As the soft-spoken mayor shows us round his domain and purrs complacently about the blessings of co-operation he is obliged to confess that the Mirs will never be happy till the Czar by a stroke of his fatherly pen shall rid them of their liabilities ; and he opens wide his blue eyes on being told that the Czar dare not do this thing. He thinks it would be the simplest affair in the world, needing nothing but to defy the Tschinn.

CHAPTER IV.

THE TEMPERANCE QUESTION.

WE have come on a flying visit to Odessa, and are living in a many-storied house, whose *dvornik* or porter is a responsible person, and we are sorry to say that he is often drunk. Sorry, because his multifarious duties require a sober mind.

He takes the rent of lodgers and gives receipts for it ; he must keep bad characters and vagabond dogs out of the house-yard ; he has to raise an alarm in case of fire, to see that the sewers are clear, to light the petroleum lamps on the staircase after dark, to scatter ashes over the pavement when it is slippery with frost, and to sweep away the snow. If he neglects any of these tasks he is liable to be fined, and even chastised in private, by the police ; yet he drinks himself incapable every feast-day, and our *istvoschik,* or coachman, gets still more drunk in his company.

Happily, coachman and porter make no pretence of attending to their duties when the boozing fit is on them. They simply vanish out of sight, and leave you to get on without them as you can. The tipsiness of the dvornik always leads to a big theft of the fuel stacked in the front yard ; that of the istvoschik obliges you to hire a public droschi, which is after all better than being driven about by a fuddled coachman, who might charge the acacias that border the dusty streets or plunge at full gallop off the quay into the port, as some have been known to do. Both the men are good, industrious fellows when sober, and express regret for their weakness ; but they have a doleful story to tell of how they once tried to become total abstainers and got into trouble with the authorities in consequence.

This was about a dozen years ago, when the liquor traffic was farmed out by Government to speculators, who abused their monopoly to sell vodki at exorbitant rates. The peasantry, knowing that there was a tariff which was only eluded by connivance with the provincial authorities, whom the monopolists bribed, banded themselves into temperance societies, with a view to forcing down the prices. Hereupon the farmers complained to Government, and the teetotal leagues were dissolved as illegal secret societies.

This had already happened in 1854 and 1859, before serfage was abolished ; and on both these

occasions very summary measures were taken towards
forcing the people to contribute to the revenue by
their intemperance.   Policemen and soldiers were
sent into the disaffected districts, and the teetotallers
were flogged into drinking ; some who doggedly held
out had liquor poured into their mouths through fun-
nels, and were afterwards hauled off to prison as
rebels ; at the same time the clergy were ordered to
preach in their churches against the new form of
sedition, and the press-censorship thenceforth laid its
veto upon all publications in which the immorality of
the liquor traffic was denounced.

These things sound incredible, but they are true.
In 1865 the people fancied that because they were no
longer serfs they could not be treated so unceremoni-
ously as of yore, but they found out their mistake.
They were simply dealt with as insurgents, and,
though not beaten, were fined, bullied, and preached
at till there was no spirit of resistance left in them.
However, this new rising led to the abolition of the
monopolies.   An excise was substituted, the price of
vodki fell by competition, and the lower orders of
Russia are now drunker than ever.   According to the
latest returns ('Wesselowski's Annual Register'), the
liquor duties yield the revenue 800,000,000 roubles
(£32,000,000 sterling) a year.

One morning a soft-spoken policeman, in a grey top-coat, calls to say that our coachman, who vanished overnight, is lying at the station under a charge of assault committed while inebriate. Is it our pleasure that he should be made to act as public scavenger for three days in the 'drunk gang'? We have a private idea that to sweep the streets would do our istvoschik no harm, but the point is really this—shall we bribe him out of his scrape, or by declining to do so stir up the police to prefer a charge which may keep him in prison, not for days, but months? We produce three roubles, reflecting that we can deduct them from Ivan Ivanowitch's wages, and by-and-by Ivan turns up, sober and thankful, to explain that he would never have been arrested at all if the police had not felt sure that his master would buy him off.

This is so true that the man will be sacred in the policeman's eyes for perhaps three months to come. Let him stagger about as rowdily as he pleases, be quarrelsome and insolent, the police will take no notice of him till the time has arrived when they think they may decently claim three more roubles.

As influential persons, such as great noblemen, bishops, diplomatic and consular agents, cannot be called upon for black-mail, their servants enjoy full

licence as to intoxication ; so do petty Civil servants
and military officers in their own persons, for a policeman who meddled with them might find himself in
trouble : but all non-official people whose servants
exceed sobriety, or who do so themselves, must bribe
or take the consequences, which are unpleasant.

A person may also be severely punished for not
getting drunk, as a certain Polish schoolmaster whom
we met one day disconsolately wielding a besom on
the quays in company of a dozen kopeckless rogues
who are being made examples of because they have
no friends.   The crime of our schoolmaster was that
he lifted up his voice in his school and in tea-shops
against ' King Vodki,' and tried to inveigle some university students into taking a temperance pledge. He
was privately warned that he had better hold his
peace, but he went on, and the result was that one
evening as he was walking home somebody bumped
against him ; he protested ; two policemen forthwith
started up, hauled him off, charged him with being
drunk and disorderly, and the next day he was sentenced to sweep the streets for three days—a sentence,
which fortunately does not involve the social annihi-
lation which it would in other countries.

The fact is that in Russia you must not advocate
temperance principles ; the vested interests in the

drink trade are too many and strong. Nobody forces you to drink yourself; the Raskolniks, or dissenters, who are the most respectable class of the Russian community and number 10,000,000 souls, are in general abstainers, but they, like others, must not overtly try to make proselytes. There are many most enlightened men who hate and deplore the national vice, who try to check it among their own servants, who would support any rational measure of legislation by which it could be diminished; but if one of them bestirred himself too actively in the matter he would find all his affairs in some mysterious fashion grow out of joint. Authors and journalists are still less in a position to cope with the evil, for the press censors systematically refuse to pass writings in which the prevalency of drunkenness is taken for granted.

Before the abolition of the monopolies a land-owner might set up a distillery on his estate, but he was compelled to sell the produce to the vodki-farmers, and these speculators might build a public-house on his land against his consent, though he was entitled to fix the spot and to receive a fair rent. At present, the trade being free, licences to distil and sell are conferred by Government (*i.e.* virtually bought of the Tschinn), and almost every landowner of consequence has one.

D

Prince Wiskoff might get one if he pleased, and has more than once thought of so doing ; but he has been deterred for want of capital to compete with his intimate enemy and neighbour, Prince Runoff, who has a distillery in full swing and floods the whole district with its produce. The Prince's chief agents are the priests, who in the farming days were allowed a regular percentage on the drink sold in their parishes, but who now receive a lump sum, nominally as an Easter gift, but on the tacit understanding that they are to push the sale of vodki by every means in their power.

The pious men do not go the length of urging their parishioners to get drunk, but they multiply the church feasts whereon revelry is the custom ; they affirm that stimulants are good for the health because of the cold climate, and they never reprove a peasant whose habitual intemperance is notorious. The Prince's land agent, the tax-collectors, the conscription officers, all join in promoting the consumption of vodki by transacting their business at the village dram-shop, with glasses before them ; and even the doctor, who lives by the Prince's patronage, prescribes vodki for every imaginable ailment.

The inducements to drink in the towns are not less than in the country. When the coachman, Ivan

Ivanowitch, goes out for a stroll among the fine streets of Odessa he is lured into the tea-shops by the loud music of barrel-organs, and vodki is served him with his tea as a matter of course. If he drives his master to a party, he has no sooner drawn up his trap under the shed in the host's yard, than the servants invite him into a lower room and give him as much spirit as he will drink; if he goes to the cornchandler's for oats, to the veterinary surgeon about his horse's legs, to the harness-maker's or coachmaker's, the preface to all business is vodki; and when he sets out to visit his kinsmen upon holidays, vodki greets him upon every threshold.

It is the same with the dvornik when he ascends to the different flats of the house to collect rent or carry letters; vodki is offered him before he has had time to state his business; and under these hospitable circumstances the wonder is not that the man should occasionally exceed sobriety, but that he should so often be sober. But in Russia a sober servant means —*exceptis excipiendis*—one who only gets drunk upon the festivals of the Church.

CHAPTER V.

THROUGH THE STREETS.

IN most Russian towns the houses are small, and every family has one of its own as in England. St. Petersburg and Odessa are exceptions.

Here the population live in flats, within six and seven storied houses, higher than those of Paris. In the poorer quarters of Odessa the giant houses have an odd look, owing firstly to the dust from the steppes, which paints them the colour of pea-soup, and secondly to the smallness of the windows and the number of absent panes which have been replaced by layers of greased paper on account of the dearness of glass.

A watch-glass costs a rouble in Odessa, a foot-square window-pane about six shillings. In the inland towns the prices are still higher; so that a Russian boy who puts his fist though a pane commits one of the heaviest crimes in the domestic decalogue and does not escape the wrath of an usually apathetic father.

Odessa enjoys the reputation of being the most Liberal city of the Empire (Moscow and Kiew being the most Conservative), and next to the capital the fairest. About ten years ago it succeeded in getting itself paved after fruitless efforts in that direction as strenuous and as remarkable in their way as those of Geneva struggling for the Protestant faith.

First a paving rate was levied in 1815, after the great peace, and the tschinovniks put the money in their pockets. Then Prince Woronzow, governor of the Chersonese, raised a new rate, but on second thoughts concluded that the money would be better spent in constructing a monumental staircase from the handsome boulevard that faces the sea down to the beach. A lean statue of the Duc de Richelieu in Roman undress stands at the top of that Babylonian flight of steps, which not a dozen persons descend in the course of the day. After this a British contractor presented himself, offering to pave the city very cheap; he bribed the tschinovniks all round, got an advance of money and disappeared.

Nothing daunted, a very intelligent golova (burgomaster) of Odessa conspired with some wealthy fellow-citizens to pave the city by a public subscription under the form of a voluntary rate ; but, having forgotten to administer douceurs in the proper

quarters, he was suspended by the civil governor
for being a meddlesome person, and the paving plans
were forwarded for the fourth time to the Office of
Public Works in St. Petersburg. The answer came
back at the end of two years, ordering the work
to be carried out by the Government engineers ; the
rate-collector went his rounds afresh, and for the next
year or two every quarterof the town was successively visited by cartloads of paving-stones.

But nothing came of these visits, except too rash
anticipations, briefly dispelled. After a cartload of
stones had encumbered a thoroughfare for a month.
another cart would come and remove it elsewhere.
Meanwhile a canopy of dust hung over the city,
obscuring the sun in fair weather, while in rainy times
the streets were often wholly impassable, certain
quarters becoming afflicted with a drought of water,
because the water-carriers could not ply their trade
either on foot or in carts. Nothing less than a visit
from the present Czar was needed to obtain for the
Odessians the great boon of getting the pavements
they had repeatedly paid for and were willing to pay
for again. So at length the city was paved ; not
cheaply, indeed, nor over well, but still paved.

These facts are worth noting, because hundreds
of other Russian towns are struggling with the

question of paving, or else with that of water supply or street-lighting, as patiently and hopelessly as Odessa did for half a century. The Czar cannot spend his life in travelling.

The streets of a Russian city are picturesque, for signboards abound and shop-fronts are painted in staring colours—light blue, yellow, and apple-green. There are no posters on hoardings, for advertising constitutes a monopoly in the hands of a company, who have hitherto confined themselves to the newspaper branch of puffing and have not mustered enterprise enough to disfigure public thoroughfares. At the corner of almost every street you come upon a Byzantine-looking shrine of the Virgin, with a number of Russians signing themselves bareheaded in front. You meet the Virgin in various other unexpected places—in railway stations, in post-offices, with a little oil-lamp flickering at her feet—even in the frowsy lock-ups, where tipsy mujicks can be heard yelling all day and night.

The behaviour of the people in the streets is quiet and civil. If a Russian knocks against you he begs your pardon with a sincere show of contrition; if he sees your nose turning white in the cold weather, he picks up a handful of snow and rubs it with brotherly officiousness till the circulation is restored.

All along the populous streets pedlars saunter selling dried mushrooms, cotton handkerchiefs, religious
prints, white bread, and *varcniches* (cheese fritters) ;
but none of them shout except the Greeks, who each
make noise enough for a dozen. Pigeons infest the
roadways with impunity, for they are held sacred ;
even if a Russian were starving it would not occur to
him to knock one of these birds on the head and cook
it. Dancing bears are also to be seen in great numbers,
and though not sacred are great favourites, and always
draw crowds, who laugh at their antics like children.

There is no man so easy to amuse as a Russian.
In the popular theatres, which stand on about the
same level as London 'penny gaffs,' he testifies his
merriment by shrieks till the tears run down his
cheeks, and it is not rare to see him in the streets
roaring before some farcical French print exposed in
a shop window. The more indecent these prints are
the better for his taste, and some windows exhibit
pictures of the kind that are reserved for the secret
albums of the dissolute in other countries. Russians are
also fanatically fond of music, and all the tea-houses
are provided with some kind of organ on the musical-
box system. These instruments are manufactured at
Moscow, and are accounted better than those of
Switzerland, the larger ones, such as enliven the big

tea-houses, playing as many as a hundred tunes and costing many hundreds of pounds. An organ of this sort makes as much noise as a full orchestra.

In the smaller tea-houses the organ tunes are frequently varied of an evening by the performance of some strolling minstrel in Caucasian costume, who strums on a triangular guitar the melodies of Lithuania and Little Russia. Very sweet melodies these are, and Chopin introduced many of them into his waltzes. The Caucasian minstrel, dressed in a black velvet tunic adorned on either breast with rows of silvered cartridge-tubes (into which he puts tobacco in time of peace), generally begins with the plaintive airs which the roussalkas (water-fairies) are supposed to sing as they lure their admirers into deep water ; he goes on by-and-by to the twanging war songs which console men for broken heads ; but as evening advances he is always called upon for a vritska, or dance, and, the tea-tables being pushed aside, the natives prepare for a hop of the wildest kind. It is a veritable French can-can, more unbridled if anything than that of the Quartier Latin ; and when joined in by Russian servant-girls with big boots and stolid faces it is irresistibly comic. Some girls, however, dance with grace and keep time to the music by rapping their heels on the floor like clog dancers.

Bells are another of the Russian's delights ; and on Sunday mornings the riot of chimes, triple peals, and bob-majors that ring from church domes is enough to gladden the most enthusiastic lover of campanology. Moscow is the place where these bells are cast, and most of them are sent to the holy city of Kiew to be blessed. A church never seems to think it has too many bells.

Thieves and policemen are the great pests of Russian towns, but especially policemen. Russians are not thieves by nature, judging by their honesty in country districts, where there are no police ; but once they get into towns the evil example set them by official persons and the venal connivance they can obtain from the police prove too tempting. A man who has resided some time in Russia even grows to doubt whether the notions of *meum* and *tuum* are comprehended there as they are in other countries. If you pay a visit and leave a cloak on the seat of your carriage, that cloak is gone when you come out. If you walk out with a dog unchained, the dog vanishes round a street corner. Shopkeepers are afraid to place articles of value in their windows. Householders are liable to have their horses and carriages stolen if they do not keep a sufficient number of stable servants, and take care to see before going to bed that one at least of these menials is sober. A man who goes out for a night-stroll unarmed may be set upon within sight of a droschky stand and stripped of every article he wears, including shirt and small clothes. The droschky drivers will not give him a helping-hand; they will rather start off altogether in a panic lest they should be summoned to give evidence; as for the police, they hurry up afterwards, and make the despoiled man pay twice the value of the things he has lost in fees for investigation.

It need scarcely be said that a person influential enough to make himself unpleasant to the police gets back his lost property in no time; the police will even restore him the equivalent if they cannot recover the actual articles. A Frenchman of rank who had left an opera-glass in a box at the Odessa opera missed it, as a matter of course, and mentioned his loss to the Civil Governor, who took up the matter forthwith. It appeared, however, that the article had been purloined by a free-lance having no connection with the police; so an official waited upon the Frenchman with a glass three times as good as the one he had lost, saying that the authorities would consider themselves disgraced if a stranger lost anything in their country—a speech which must have given the Frenchman a rosy idea of Russian honesty.

Merchants and tradesmen often pay thief-insurance money to the police ; but as the thieves can generally afford to pay still more for the privilege of being let alone, the insurance is only accepted *ad valorem*, so to say. For instance, a man may insure his watch, great-coat, and dog, but not his safe if burglars can manage to rifle it. Besides, the police do not play fair, and continually shield themselves by pretending that there are too many independent rogues about who meanly work on their own sole account. One comfort is that the Russian who waylays and strips you seldom does you bodily injury. He is a gentle thief, who pulls off your furred boots as considerately as if they were his own which you had put on by mistake. It takes time to accustom oneself to Russian character ; but you end by learning that the Russian appears in his softest light when he is bettering himself in some way at your expense.

Improbable as it may sound, governors of gaols often let out prisoners on purpose that they may thieve. Last year the Moscow papers reported the case of a celebrated burglar, who, having been lodged in the penitentiary, was one night caught 'cracking the crib' of a wealthy merchant. This led to inquiries, and the burglar confessed that, having planned his robbery before entering gaol, he had spoken about it to one of the turnkeys, who had let him out on condition of going with him and sharing the proceeds. The turnkey did not deny this, but said he had acted under instructions from the governor, who had bargained to have the lion's share. The governor in his turn tried to throw the blame on the police, alleging that they had given him orders to let out the prisoner for some purpose not stated; but the story was disbelieved and the governor was dismissed. Soon afterwards the burglar was tried by a jury and acquitted, but the turnkey was not even indicted.

CHAPTER VI.

THE BRISKATSTARTINE HUSSARS.

IN a number of villages dotted about over the steppe within a dozen versts of Odessa, troops and half-troops of the Briskatstartine Hussars were quartered before the war. It is the custom to station Russian cavalry in villages because of the facilities for getting forage.   There is a cavalry barrack inside Odessa which serves as depôt, and where at this moment a major of the Briskatstartines is drilling and clothing droves of shy tow-haired recruits sent to him from as far as Esthonia, Livonia, Jaroslav, and Arkhangelsk for consignment to the seat of war.

This major we shall call Strengmann. He is a half-German from Courland—poor, hardworked, as good a soldier as ever wore spurs, but one who will never rise above his present grade, because he fulfils its duties too well and because he is not a nobleman. An officer does not count in Russian society until he reaches the rank of lieutenant-colonel ; and, though the son of a high-class *tschinovnik* must pass for form's sake through the subaltern grades, he is generally detached on staff duty till he can be hoisted to the rank befitting his birth. Strengmann's colonel, Prince Topoff, is just twenty-eight; the lieutenant-colonel, Prince Tripoff, recently kept his twenty-sixth birthday, between two defeats near Kars.

Strengmann was never on familiar terms with these gentlemen, who lived in high state in houses of their own at Odessa and who treated him with courteous haughtiness. They never invited him to dinner, and he did not expect they should. Strengmann has never sat at an aristocratic table in his life. When he went to make his reports to Topoff or Tripoff he usually found them in bed, sleepy after an agreeable night's baccarat at the Club of Nobles. They would keep him standing while he told his business, then sign his reports without a word, and dismiss him with a nod. On reviews and other gala occasions the two princes used to figure at the head of their regiment in glittering uniforms of sky-blue and silver; but at other times the management of the regiment, in all but financial matters, was left wholly in Strengmann's hands. The finances Prince Topoff managed with his private steward, as the custom is among Russian colonels. It was in keeping with these arrangements that when the war broke out and a chance of glory appeared Topoff and Tripoff should have been sent off to take it, while Strengmann remained behind.

To be sure, if the elegant Topoff and the fascinating Tripoff had been relegated to depôt duty they could never have succeeded as Strengmann does in co-ordinating the polyglot elements of which a Russian regiment is composed. As a matter of policy natives of the north are sent into regiments quartered south, and *vice versâ*. Soldiers are also sorted, as far as possible, according to their size and complexion. Under Nicholas there was a hussar regiment altogether made up of dark-haired men pitted with the small-pox, and another of light-haired men in the same case. There was a regiment whose soldiers all had fair hair, slim figures, and blue eyes; and another where swarthy features and eagle noses were the rule.

These happy assortments have been less strictly adhered to under the present reign, but enough is done in the way of sizing to bring men of twenty different dialects into each regiment, and thereby greatly to obviate the risks of mutiny. Strengmann knows a few dozen words out of every language spoken from the Oural Mountains to the Caucasus, and when he cannot piece a whole sentence together he makes up for deficient parts of speech with so many strokes from a cane which he is always switching behind his back. He ought not to beat his soldiers, but he does, because he has found out that cane is the only tongue universally understood. His adjutant, depôt-captain, and lieutenant have likewise made this discovery. So have the sergeants and corporals; and, as there is no one to prevent all these officers from conducting discipline in their own way, they deal their blows right and left.

One word about blows in Russia. A nobleman who should strike a mujick or a soldier in anger would be obliged to pay a sum of money to escape the consequences, which might be serious. Since the Emancipation a ukase has abolished the knout, the rattan, and even the birch in State schools. Noblemen have been especially ordered to abstain from assaults; and an infringement of this rule, if not compounded by the victim, might lead to the nobleman being degraded from his rank in the Tschinn by the marshal of the nobility in his district. But mujicks continue to pummel one another, and to be pummelled by their superiors who are not of noble blood, for this is custom. The policeman thumps the droschky-driver, and the driver thumps the ostler; the ostler thumps the beggar, and the beggar thumps whom he can.

E

Blows cause no bad blood. Strengmann thwacks his soldiers without mercy but without wrath, and they yell without stint but without rancour.

Here is a long-haired Livonian who is bleating like a calf in the barrack-yard because he has been taken away from his village, which he will not see again for a dozen years. What would be the use of sending him to snooze in the guard-room? A few touches with the cane serve the much more practical purpose of despatching him skipping towards the barber, who will clip his poll and pass him on to the clothing sergeant, who will rig him out in boots and a grey coat which will engross his attention for the rest of the day.

Here, again, are a batch of soldiers who have slept out of barracks and been brought in drunk; and another batch who are being dragged in by the police for looting in shops. Expostulation would be of no use, and imprisonment, if systematically applied, would soon have the effect of clearing out the barracks. So the major's awful cane is set going, and the culprits make no complaints.

The soldiers like Strengmann fairly well, and he is good to them after a fashion, like that of a keeper with young bears. He knows that soldiers must get drunk, for they have nothing else to do, and must loot, for they have often not enough to eat. Their barracks is a fearful place of stenches, mouldiness, and dirt. The soldiers have no bedding, but sleep on wooden cots wrapped up in their cloaks. Their food is *tchi*, served twice a day with an occasional lump of beef in it, and a pound of black bread, ill-baked, because damp bread weighs more than dry and brings so much profit to the baker.

On pay-day a soldier is supposed to receive one or two kopecks; but the majority of them are on permanent stoppages because of articles of their kit which they have sold to buy drink with, or because of alleged barrack damages committed while drunken. As not one soldier in a hundred can read, the account-book which the paymaster fills up for him every month is a volume of cryptography; and he can be made to pay for a pair of boots a dozen times over without being any the wiser. When by chance an atom of pay is doled out it goes to the canteen immediately. So does the money which a soldier can earn by picking up an odd job or two by working for landowners or tradesmen in towns.

Nothing can stop a soldier from accepting these jobs with or without leave. Sometimes in harvest a regiment will melt clean away, and scouts will be employed for a month in riding after the runaways

and whipping them back to barracks like a pack of
straggling hounds.   More commonly, however, the
colonel, or rather his steward, contracts for hiring out
a few hundred men at a time for harvesting, and puts
two-thirds of the money into his pocket.   The other
third comes to him through the canteen, which is his
property.   It is the colonel who clothes, feeds, and
pays his regiment and keeps the barracks in repair;
so perhaps Prince Topoff's steward would be able
to explain how the bread, boots, and barracks of the
Briskatstartine Hussars are such sorry things, and
how the soldier's pay generally comes to nothing as
above said.

If a stranger visit the barracks of the Preobajentski
Guards at St. Petersburg he will see quarters which
are all that such places should be.   The rooms shine
with kaolin varnish, the men's kits are magnificent,
the rations are of good weight and wholesome, the
drains emit no odours, and pay comes in regularly.
But then the Czar often visits the barracks of his favourite regiment, which have become a show-place for
foreigners.

And every time the Czar announces his intention
of visiting another barrack that place immediately
becomes a show too.   When his Majesty went to
Odessa the Colonel of the Briskatstartines spent se-

veral thousand pounds in making his men and their
quarters look sumptuous. For three days the soldiers
lived in clover—new clothes, good dinners, money in
their pockets, vodki to drink, and clean rugs to lie
down upon. No wonder their loyalty was pleasantly
stimulated towards the Sovereign whose presence
could conjure up such blessings; but as soon as the
well-intentioned but not ubiquitous monarch had
turned his back things relapsed into their old groove,
which is one of squalor. The money that is set down
in the estimates for the keep of a regiment is amply
sufficient if it reached its destination; but a part somehow sticks in the War-Office; another lump gets lost
between the fingers of the general commanding the
division; the brigade general next mislays a portion;
finally the colonel comes, who thinks he should be a
zany if he did not levy his due commission upon the
remainder.

The impulse thus given from above extends to the
lowest officer who is entrusted with a single rouble
for regimental use. Major Strengmann filches all he
can because he does not get his pay regularly; the
captain follows suit, and the sergeant-major plays the
same card. The surgeon who directs the infirmary
sends in a long bill for medicines, and gives his
patients vodki, which cures them quite as well. The

quartermaster pockets the money that should go to mend the drains ; the adjutant gets a bonus from the contractors who supply rotten wheat and tainted meat.

Say that from fire or some other cause a part of the barracks becomes so damaged as to require repair. The quartermaster estimates the cost at 10 per cent. more than is needed, the major claps on 10 per cent. more, the colonel another 10 per cent., and so on till the War Office is reached. Here the tschinovniks, having taxed the bill, allow about two-thirds of the sum asked (though they enter the whole on their books), and the money passing through the series of hands already mentioned eventually reaches the quartermaster under the form of a trifle not sufficient for the purpose in hand. So the repairs are effected in a shoddy fashion, if at all; and some day one hears that a high wind has blown down a whole wing of the barracks, and killed two or three score of men in it.

But there is no free press to take note of these things, so the old game goes on. Those who remember how the British soldier was robbed not more than forty years ago, when newspapers were already pretty plainspoken, may reckon what chances there are of the Russian military administration being improved under a system of government which is about a hundred years behind what the English circumlocution departments were in 1830. Meanwhile, the Russian soldier is not discontented in the midst of his filth and hardships. He plods on like one who is undergoing man's fated lot, and in war he fights like a hero for the men who plunder him, happy if he can win a copper medal with a smart ribbon which he will sport when he goes back to his village to the admiration of his somnolent, ill-washed sweetheart.

CHAPTER VII.

A VICTORIOUS GENERAL.

ONE of Prince Topoff's predecessors in the colonelcy of the Briskatstartine Hussars was Prince Falutinski, now general, and commonly known as the hero of the Daghestan war. He is a splendid-looking personage, six feet high, well whiskered, and not yet fifty. He is perfumed with musk and wears two or three diamond rings. His eyes are soft and his manners charming : he has been employed in diplomacy, he has been governor of a province, he is a privy councillor, and acted for a while as manager-general of the Imperial theatres. No man is appointed to this high post who has not first proved his science on fields of battle ; and General Falutinski is universally admitted to have displayed at once ·tact and courage in his delicate duties of engaging Italian prime-donne and French comics. It is only a captious mind that could contend there is anything unmilitary in such functions. General Falutinski, in his glittering uniform all covered with stars, was much more potent in maintaining harmony among rival songstresses than any puny civilian could have been ; and as to the fiddlers in the orchestra, who but a general could have made these gentlemen tremble in their shoes when they once threatened to strike because of an unpopular conductor ?

But every man, except the Czar, has his failings, and the general had once, perhaps, the defect of bragging too much. It was not, however, the ponderous pragmatical brag which makes victorious Germans so offensive, nor yet that vapouring French bombast which is so easy to see through. It was brag which those hearing it took for solid truth. The General impressed everybody with a sense of his country's power and of his own unlimited worth ; he appeared to be earnest and thoughtful ; one fancied, after listening to him, that Russia was exercising a wonderful self-control in not launching her legions to subjugate all opponents of her philanthropic policy.

Philanthropy and Russian policy were in Falutinski's mouth convertible terms. He ecstatized innumerable journalists and sentimental politicians by means of them ; he even succeeded in puzzling some second-rate statesmen, who were more pervious to his personal fascination than alive to the interests of the countries they were paid to serve. Russia never commits the mistake of getting her foreign business transacted by square-toed respectability. Falutinski had the well-bred haughtiness which keeps the vulgar at a distance, the grace in trifling which pleases women, and that affable art of appearing to be confidential which dupes persons on the look-out for ' early information '—to be used in Parliament, on 'Change, or in the press.

Among all who could serve him by influencing public opinion the General squandered the small coin of courtesy and kind words most lavishly; so that he never went anywhere without making himself a useful friend or two. Besides, his interlocutors were always bound to remember that he was the great Falutinski of the Daghestan war—not a commonplace person by any means, nor one who could be suspected of brag. He had led his victorious army over the sand plains of Anketer, had crossed the swollen river Terek in face of a murderous fire, and routed the hordes of the fierce Bagallyou Khan in their fastnesses. Special correspondents had written in the most laudatory terms of these acts of valour and skill ; and these independent observers have so much to do with the making of military reputations nowadays that it was no wonder Falutinski should have been classed high in the estimation of the world and in his own.

He was not observed to study strategy in his leisure
hours, for he was too busy with diplomatists and
opera-singers as above said ; and it was not even
proved that he had ever read military books in his
youth, for he was a colonel at twenty-five, and had
till then chiefly distinguished himself by leading the
cotillons at Court balls. But a man who has innate
military genius need not pour over books as Von
Moltke does ; and when riding on horseback at the
State reviews in the Admiralty Square of St. Petersburg Falutinski looked the very beau-idéal of a warrior.
Indeed, if he and Von Moltke had been placed side
by side, women, who are known to be infallible judges
of masculine character, would have had no hesitation
in deciding which of the two was best fitted to lead
soldiers to victory.

The plain truth is, however, that the Daghestan
war was one of those Russian military games of which
outsiders do not always see most. We forget how
long ago this philanthropic crusade took place, and
for what precise reason it was that Bagallyou Khan
incurred the wrath of the Holy Empire ; but the man
had to be chastised, and the Grand Duke Rurik was
sent to do it. He chose Falutinski, his boon friend,
as chief of the staff, and with an army of 30,000 men,
ever so many guns, and a dozen hospitably enter-

tained correspondents, marched to the shores of the Caspian Sea, where Bagallyou Khan smote him hip and thigh.

But this was only the outset of the campaign, and the world heard little of the defeat; for the Grand Duke courteously informed the correspondents that he would prefer they should not report Russian failures for the present, owing to State reasons. The correspondents thought this request most reasonable. It was made to them with very good grace after a dinner in the Grand Duke's tent, and Falutinski, as they well knew, had charge of the post-office through which their letters must have gone.

Meanwhile, the Grand Duke sent off to St. Petersburg an account of his first battle, in which he forgot to mention that he had been beaten; so that a Cabinet courier arrived, bringing decorations and other honours for him and Falutinski just as they had finished fighting their second battle, in which they were more badly worsted than the first time. In this second disastrous affair the Grand Duke's kitchen battery was captured, along with his French cook; and rumours came from the enemy's camp of atrocities committed on this foreigner, who had been made to swallow six quarts of the soup he had prepared for the ducal table.

It now turned out that his Imperial Highness
and his staff commander had erred through not being
very clear as to their geography.   They had mis-
taken the exact position of a river, a chain of mountains, or something of that sort ; so that having
made a gallant dash onwards they found themselves
upon a sand plain of several hundred miles in extent,
instead of in the heart of the enemy's country as they
had imaginatively hoped.

The Grand Duke Rurik, who was a brave young
man, very headstrong and sentimental, was for push-
ing on over the plain to be beaten again and die ; but
Falutinski, though equally courageous, opined that
it would be better to conquer and live.   He knew
that Russia, having once begun the war, would go
on with it regardless of cost ; and thought he might
as well finish it by hook or crook as leave the credit
to some other general.   So the correspondents were
told to be patient, for the end was not yet ; and Falutinski held numerous councils with the Grand Duke,
after which, in the dead of the night, parliamentarians
were sent off with a flag of truce to Bagallyou Khan's
camp.

Soon an armistice was announced ; Falutinski was
missed for a few days, and the correspondents learned
that he had gone in person to carry an ultimatum to

the barbarous chief demanding of him an uncon-
ditional surrender.   One bright morning, however, he
returned, declaring that Bagallyou Khan would not
hear reason, and once more preparations were made
for a grand set-to.

Somehow, though, from the time of Falutinski's
visit to the Khan things began to go badly with that
barbarian's army.   His soldiers left off guarding an
important ford ; some others were surprised by a force
ten times superior to them, and were cut to pieces ;
another detachment who should have held a mountain
pass got into the wrong pass by error, and, being
attacked in the rear, had to capitulate.

The correspondents now began to write home in
fine style. Falutinski's strategy was extolled as a thing
at once deep and beautiful. The Russian soldiers,
decimated by the previous encounters, but ever doggedly brave, picked up fresh heart, and one morning
Europe heard with feelings of wonder and admiration
of Falutinski's glorious march over the plains of
Anketer.

It is always grand to see a soldier surmounting
natural obstacles ; but, according to the strategists
who reviewed Falutinski's proceedings on paper, no
general ever had defied drought, heat, mosquitoes, and
savages with such a combination of tactical wisdom

and devil-may-care recklessness as he. Then came
the final pitched battle on the river Terek, where the
flower of Bagallyou Khan's army bit the dust by
moonlight. It was a thunderlike stroke of genius,
wrote the correspondents. The valiant general fell
upon the infidels like Sennacherib, started them out
of sleep, hewed, slew, and pulverized them, ultimately
scattering their remnants as dust in a high wind.

In this historic fight the Grand Duke recovered
his kitchen battery and French cook. There was
glory enough and to spare for all. Six standards,
the sacred kettle of the tribe, and four of Bagallyou
Khan's plumpest wives were among the spoil; but
the chief himself was not to be found, to the great
regret of all concerned.

He turned up a few months later at St. Petersburg.
Then it was learned that he had not come as an im-
pertinent rebel with bristling moustache, but as a
humble suppliant for Imperial grace, confessing his
sins and stedfastly purposing to lead a new life.
Accordingly, a grand levée was appointed for his
public obeisance, and his victors, the Grand Duke
Rurik and General Falutinski, stood on either side of
the throne upon the solemn occasion. All present
were much touched to see the proud Khan walk in
erect with the dignity of misfortune, and, bending his

knee before the throne, make a gesture as of heartfelt readiness to let his head be chopped off; but he was graciously bidden to rise, and Muscovite clemency was carried to the point of allowing him a high rank in the Imperial service, a palace on the Neva, and a handsome pension to keep up his state.

He became a devoted subject after that, and, adapting himself to the civilization of the West as well as to the religion of his conquerors, drank champagne like a true Christian and learned to play whist. It is pleasant to add that he and his old enemy Falutinski lived on terms of mutual esteem and friendship as became valorous men. They did not speak much when they met, but an almost imperceptible contraction in their left eyelids testified to that inner emotion which proceeds from the contact of natures fitted to understand and admire each other.

The moral of this little story is that diplomacy is no bad adjunct to force in certain campaigns.

CHAPTER VIII.

A PROSPEROUS MERCHANT.

IN one of the dingiest *percouloks*, or slums, of Odessa stands the office of Simon Iscariotivitch, a Jew worth several millions of roubles. His private house is situated in a finer quarter of the city, and he transacts business there too as a money-lender.

His sources of income are multifarious, and he calls himself vaguely a merchant, without saying merchant of what. He belongs to the first class of the Commercial Guild. Merchants of this first class have to declare a capital of £2,400, and to pay a yearly licence of £105 12s. (600 roubles); those of the second declare a capital of £920, and pay £42 4s. 10d; and those of the third are supposed to be worth £384, and pay £12 11s. 2d. Beneath these three guilds there is a class of petty traders who pay from £3 to £4 a year—a heavy tax to many of them; and you might suppose Simon Iscariotivitch to belong to this last category, if you judged by the shabbiness of his office.

F

But Simon is often absent from Odessa, travelling among the *pomeschiks* (landowners on the steppes) ; and it is in the course of these visits to the squires that he gets through most of his business, which requires no showy counting-house. He is a small snuffling man dressed in what looks like a decayed dressing-gown and in flat, round hat scabby with age. He sells tea, French novels, agricultural machinery, vodki, silk, turquoises, pianos, and musical boxes ; and he buys corn, wool, horses, and ponies. A little transaction which he had two years ago with Prince Wiskoff will explain one of his favourite methods of assisting aristocrats in difficulties and bettering himself at the same time.

One scorching summer day, when the Prince was drowsy from heat and ennui, the Jew's *telega*, dusty from travel, scampered into the courtyard of the ramshackle palace. A visit of any sort is so pleasant to a rusticating prince that he would welcome a creditor sooner than see nobody ; and Serge Wiskoff, who knew Simon right well, saw many a reason to rejoice at his coming. However, he maintained the dignity befitting a Christian in the presence of an infidel ; and Simon, having humbly kissed his hand, proceeded by circumlocutory methods to hint that he was ready to buy the Prince's crop of standing corn.

The Prince was equally ready to sell it him, and the following year's crop as well. Simon took time to consider, but at length said he would buy next year's crop too. Then the Prince said, 'Why not buy three, four, five years' crops?' And so the pair haggled till, by dint of coaxing supplications on the Prince's part and steady but doleful bargaining on the Jew's, who swore he should be ruined, Simon eventually agreed to take five years' crops at something like a third of their value in the market.

The Prince was greatly excited, for the sum offered was enough to allow of his starting at once for Paris with his wife and having a year's fun there—the only thing on earth for which he cared. Accordingly a printed form of agreement was extracted from Simon's greasy travelling bag, the Prince filled it up and appended his signature, whereupon Simon, having taken possession of the document, drew from the inner breast-pocket of his blue *kaftan*, not a roll of bank-notes, but a parcel of the Prince's dishonoured bills from divers Western capitals, which he restored to their owner with an obsequiousness most cringing.

The disappointment was awful, and the Prince used bad language; the barina, too, who had come into the room and had already commenced building French hotels in the air, clenched her plump hands and talked of having the infidel tallyman whipped off the estate. But Simon was lamentably humble : no creature alive can be so humble as a Russian Jew. He had bought the bills for good money, whined he, knowing that a Wiskoff's bond was worth gold, and he was sure their high nobilities would believe that he had thought to render them a real service in acting as he had done. Their high nobilities were in a vile temper, but they had to submit. There was luckily a residue to be paid in real money—two thousand roubles or so—which consoled them for their misadventure by giving them the wherewithal to live high and fast for six weeks, which they religiously did.

But Simon's profits on this affair were not ended here. In the ensuing August a long caravan of carts set out from the Prince's estate, carrying the corn to Odessa. The Prince's steward, a sly, flat-nosed Kalmuck, had charge of the carts ; and he and Simon were in league, having had a secret and mutually agreeable interview before the corn was bought. So it somehow befell that the caravan tarried on its road, then got lost in a steppe fog, then went many scores of versts out of its way, and finally was overtaken by the September rains, which spoiled a good half of the wheat. Moreover, when Odessa was reached it was raining still, and there were no barns to be let.

Simon and the Kalmuck walked down to the port together, and satisfied themselves as to this fact. Meanwhile the caravan, with its oxen and peasants, could not be left to take care of itself in the streets, where the police were already flocking to levy blackmail of the carters for obstructing the thoroughfare ; so the Kalmuck was fain to beg that the Jew would find him a store-house on any terms, which the Jew kindly did by procuring him a barn of his own which had been empty all the while, as the Kalmuck well knew. The next thing to do was to sift the good wheat from the bad, for the Jew had not agreed to buy damaged corn. He had covenanted for the number of quarters of wheat which the Prince's crops were supposed to yield, not for the crops as they stood, and it had further been agreed that the corn should be delivered within some covered building ; hence the necessity for the Kalmuck's getting a barn.

When the corn had been inspected all that was not up to sample was naturally declined, and the question arose as to what should be done with the damaged quantity ? The Kalmuck readily decided that it was of no use to carry it back to the estate, and still less expedient to pay for keeping it stored in Odessa ; so, upon Simon's offering to buy it for a small sum as pigs' food, he accepted the small sum, privily minded to give no account of the same to his master, but to declare that the damaged corn had been thrown into the sea by order of some market inspectors. As for Simon, he gave nothing to the pigs, but, shipping the damaged wheat on to a worthless vessel, insured the cargo as good corn, and gave the Greek captain orders to run himself ashore—which was done, and Simon pocketed the insurance money.

On the whole, it will be seen that the honest merchant played his cards well. Prince Wiskoff, having been unable to fulfil his engagement towards him with one year's crop, was obliged to make up the deficit (6 per cent. interest added) with next year's; but, as the next year brought fresh accidents which saddled him again with arrears, it came to pass that in parting with five years' harvests he was found to have virtually alienated eight, if not ten.

Simon Iscariotivitch does many other strokes of business in this fashion. For instance, he purchases sheep of the *pomeschiks*, and, having contrived with the stewards that a good number of them should be brought to Odessa diseased, buys these last for a trifle, as he did the bad corn, and sells them as prime mutton (by agreement with military authorities) to feed the Briskatstartine Hussars and other valiant regiments. He is also great at purchasing spavined ponies, which

turn out to have not so much the matter with them
once they get into his hands ; and ugly knock-kneed
colts, which the *pomeschiks*, who sold them cheap, have
the pleasure of seeing by-and-by spanking about the
Boulevard of Odessa as first-rate Orloff trotters.

In fact, Simon trades upon the incurable repugnance of Russian gentlemen to looking after their
landed interests, and if his profits be so great the fault
is theirs. He is a curious, shambling man, whose
sharpness in business is set off by a humility of
demeanour difficult to describe and painful to witness.
He fawns before a nobleman as if he were afraid of
being kicked, and in this resembles most of his
Russian co-religionists who are past middle age and
have retained a scaring recollection of the days when
kicking and cuffing were their common lot and when
the law oppressed them with grinding disabilities.

Up to the death of Nicholas Jews were not allowed
to possess land, to give evidence in civil suits, to have
synagogues, nor to inhabit the holy cities of Kiew and
Moscow. They were obliged to wear a particular
dress, and out of every Jewish family one child was
always taken by the State to be educated as a Christian at his parents' cost.

It requires more than one lifetime to outlive the
remembrance of such social inferiority, even when the

law has removed it. Simon Iscariotivitch has now his synagogues, his Jewish schools, his municipal privileges, and he is suffered to celebrate the festivals of his Church with public displays ; and if anybody kicked him it would be a bad thing for the kicker. Sometimes a band of riotous university students in their cups will try their hands at the old game of assaulting a Jew, whereon that Jew begins to howl, and all the other Jews within earshot howl too, till, the streets being filled with their uproar, the culprits are summarily punished by a police-judge, in order that tranquillity may be restored. This howling device has been found of great protection to the long-suffering community ; but, though it secures the Jews against ill-treatment, nothing has been able to diminish the contempt felt for them by all classes of Russians, but especially by the upper.

They still labour under many disabilities not within the law. Simon's wealth is enormous, but he cannot hope to be ennobled. The nobles will not admit him to their clubs nor to their houses as a guest ; they would leave their stalls at the opera if he came and sat down among them ; they would not dine at his house for any consideration ; and if he were to send his sons into the army no exertions on his part and no amount of merit on that of the young Iscariotivitchs would enable these latter to rise higher than subaltern's rank.

As a consequence, Simon and his brethren hate the Tschinn with a bitterness all the more dangerous as two-thirds of the trade of Southern Russia, and at least one-third of that in the North, is in their hands. Being virtually tabooed from public functions, they have no public spirit ; and, holding no land, they do not care what befalls the soil and the haughty lords of it. The large sums of specie amassed by them are invested out of the country, and do nothing to promote native industry ; but of late years they have begun to show themselves alive to the political uses of wealth, and it is more than suspected that most of the agrarian agitation which is making the peasant minds simmer is subsidized by Jews.

Simon Iscariotivitch never goes on his travelling rounds without dropping into the ears of peasants cunning theories which would have caused him to be hanged twenty-five years ago, and which even now would bring him to trouble if there were any shorthand writer present to take them down. At this time of war Simon contributes his share towards promoting popular distress and discontent by refusing to accept Government paper for less than 30 per cent. discount. He predicts in whispers a national bankruptcy, and will not advance a bank-note to impecunious nobles on bills or land mortgage, but only on such portable security as plate and diamonds. Exclusive laws and fanatical prejudices have made him an alien on Russian soil, and he acts as aliens ever do among a hostile people.

CHAPTER IX.

JUDICIAL BUSINESS.

THE first article of the French Civil Code says, 'No man is supposed to be ignorant of the law.' If a Russian were expected to know the laws of his country he would have to master twenty-one folio volumes, containing some 2,000 pages apiece. But, then, in Russia every conceivable act of man is regulated by Imperial decree.

Whenever some influential tschinovnik has found his private affairs disordered by the advance of progress, he has procured an Imperial ukase to bar that progress. There are laws regulating the cut of one's beard, the fashion of one's hat and coat ; a man cannot light a cigar in the streets without peril of infringing some decree which might be enforced against him by any rich man desirous of getting him into trouble. In other countries everything that the law does not forbid is allowed ; in Russia everything is forbidden which the law does not expressly permit.

People get out of this predicament by purchasing as much liberty as they require for their individual use, as Englishmen do gas and water. If the decrees were stringently enforced no man could breathe ; but the system of corruption serves as a check upon compression, just as smuggling does upon prohibitive tariffs. The Baltic Provinces are the only parts of the empire where the administrative screw is systematically pressed down to the grinding of men's souls ; for Germans are formidable bureaucrats, and find more delight in making themselves disagreeable than in being bribed. But here despotism is tempered by the frequent assassination of tschinovniks, and the country is so profoundly disaffected that it will seize upon the first convenient opportunity for getting annexed to Germany. Everywhere else where the pure-bred, lazy, venal Russian sits in places of power a man jogs on fairly well till he crosses another man with a longer purse ; then he goes to the wall.

There is no mistake about this ; it is the unwritten law which dominates over all the printed edicts in the twenty-one-volumed code. A tschinovnik who has a quarrel with another tschinovnik does not think of going to law about it ; he refers the dispute to the marshal of the nobility in his district, and this official, assisted, if need be, by the standing committee of

nobles, arbitrates in private—sometimes equitably,
sometimes not, according as there may or may not be
reasons for putting the less influential party in the
wrong.

But when a tschinovnik falls out with an ordinary
citizen, then one of two things occurs : either the
tschinovnik's order stands by him, in which case the
other party collapses, or he is left to fight his own
battle ; and then it becomes a question whether he
can make head against an opponent who probably has
an artel, or mutual relief society, behind him.

Almost every Russian exercising a trade or profession belongs to an artel. The droschky drivers
have one, so have the tea-house waiters. The Jews
form an artel by themselves, besides belonging to their
respective trade artels ; and they are the toughest
opponents of all, from their loyalty in standing by
one another. The Tschinn would not care to make
common cause with one of its members who had a suit
concerning private matters with a rich Jew ; the
nobleman would rather be advised to compromise the
quarrel, and would take the hint.

Jews seldom go to law with one another : if im-
pleaded by Russians of the trading class, they win by
force of money. If two Christian traders go before
the courts it must be for spite, for they well know that

a suit will cost both of them ten times more than a
private agreement. Bribes are not handed direct to
the judges, but conveyed through the notaries—an
astute corporation. A judge of first instance, commonly a tschinovnik, is paid £40 a year, and has bought
his office secretly for about £4,000. His income consequently depends on his perquisites; and he must
use the scales of justice in no metaphorical sense to
weigh on which side the roubles lie. Like Lord Bacon,
all these Russian judges might contend that they sell
justice, not injustice; for whichever way they may
decide they have some Imperial decree to rest upon;
and if their judgments be quashed by a court of appeal,
that court has law on its side too. A civil suit is, in
fact, an auction in which the highest bidder prevails
on the judge to select from the code the decree which
he requires to put him in the right.

Foreigners, when they first come to settle in the
country, are very apt to be dragged into lawsuits by
people who want to extort money from them. If a
man resists the imposition, bribes a judge to uphold
him, and so gets boldly out of the scrape, he is likely
to be let alone for the future, just as in duelling
countries a man who has stood fire once is said to
have *fait ses preuves.*

In criminal causes defendants fare according to

the animosity and wealth of the persons who prosecute them. Russian judges have a kindly feeling for petty thieves, and, if not paid to punish them severely, can easily be cajoled into passing a light sentence. But, of course, a prisoner who throws himself upon the mercy of the court must be perfectly destitute ; for, if he were to hire an advocate without having bribed the judge, the latter would naturally make him smart for the oversight. The mistake is scarcely possible, however ; for an attorney would take care that the prisoner spent his money rightly. A judge can be bribed to acquit, but if he have been already bribed to convict he can be bribed to pass a light sentence ; or if he be pledged to inflict a heavy penalty, then the attorney would advise his client to save his money, in order to bribe himself out of prison, or, failing that, to procure himself relaxations therein.

Juries only sit in cases of felony and of the worst crimes of violence ; and they too are amenable to bribery and sentiment. He must be a dull advocate who cannot make a Russian jury weep. The well-known story of a jury who acquitted a prisoner because it was Easter eve, and they thought they could best solemnize the holy week by forgiving transgressions, can be capped by another of an Odessa jury who acquitted a wife-murderer because the deceased had beaten him for being tipsy. It has passed into a proverb that it is safer to kill a rich man outright than to maim him ; for if alive he can pursue his vengeance himself, whereas if he be dead his heirs may forget to spend money in assuring the conviction of the murderer, who thereupon escapes by pleading provocation.

In a general way it is the rich who by their prosecutions keep the prisons and penal colonies of Siberia populated ; and they are terrible persons to offend in person or property. The civil and criminal laws are so intermuddled that a breach of contract, a trespass, or a mere debt may be construed into a felony at the suit of a vindictive tschinovnik ; and malice would be wreaked in manifold and horrible ways but for the artels which protect the poor. As it is, an artel has occasionally to spend enormous sums of money in rescuing an innocent member from what would in any other country be deemed a frivolous and vexatious prosecution.

In the country districts the peasantry have a remedy against this sort of thing by burning down the houses and ricks of the landowners who oppress them ; and they are so prompt to do this that a nobleman who is brutal towards townspeople becomes quite mild among his peasantry.

Domestic servants are the worst sufferers from

plutocratic spite, for, while most liable to give offence, they are defenceless, having no artels. There is an artel of cooks and another of coachmen in St. Petersburg, but footmen, maids, and valets have to take care of themselves. A confidential servant incurs the wrath of his master and finds himself arrested one morning on the easily proved charge of stealing. The fact that all servants steal, and that the culprit had been stealing for years before his master condescended to notice it, is of course not accepted as an excuse ; and it depends entirely on the master's readiness to bribe whether the poor wretch is sent to Siberia on the count of major felony or consigned to prison as a petty rogue. But if the minor count be admitted the valet soon discovers that his master's power over him does not cease at the prison doors. By gilding the palm of the prison governor the master can have his domestic whipped for alleged breaches of gaol discipline, till the miserable fellow becomes supple as a glove and bewails the day when he was saucy. Great ladies sometimes try this curative system on their maids, and more than one French soubrette in St. Petersburg has discovered in prison what it costs to trade upon the secrets of a Russian *grande dame's* boudoir.

That prisons should exist in Russia for the punishment of murderers and maimers is conceivable ; but, when one considers that peculation is the very mainspring of all business in the country, it certainly seems odd that any judge should have the face to imprison a thief. Possibly the authorities are struck with the incongruity of this arrangement, for whenever the Czar travels he releases prisoners wholesale ; and these discharged ragamuffins are welcomed by the population as though they were brothers whose only crime had been ill-luck.

A curious thing it is to see a Russian court of justice during the trial of criminal cases. The judges are in uniform and wear the medals or stars of some civil order of knighthood on their breasts. The counsel wear uniforms too in their capacity as subalterns in the legal hierarchy. It looks to a foreigner as if he were witnessing a court martial in which the thief was being tried by field marshals and defended by a captain. The jury are tradesmen or petty squires, but it often happens that the majority can neither read nor write. They kneel when being sworn ; and give free rein to their emotions while the witnesses are deposing. The judges have to threaten them with fines when they all begin shouting ' Oh ! ' and ' Ah ! ' together. Their distaste for convicting is so great that they will frequently sing out to a prisoner : 'Will you promise not to do it again ?' Once when a jury had been locked up three hours an impatient judge sent an usher to see what they were doing, and it was found that they had all escaped through a window, to avoid giving a verdict.

CHAPTER X.

FORGED BANK-NOTES.

IN the town of K——, of the province of Kharkov, Otto, the son of Herr Dicker, hotel-keeper, one morning received a parcel of forged bank-notes, in payment for a tun of Crimean wine supplied to the venerable Archimandrite. Forged notes are as common as genuine ones in Russia, and if Herr Dicker had been a Russian he would have simply passed on the notes to some one else.

Being a German, it behoved him to be cautious. First he scolded his son for not having scrutinized the water-marks; after which he pondered for a while whether he should treat the transaction as a dead loss, or go to the Archimandrite's majordomo, who had paid the notes, and ask him for others.

He had the misfortune to choose the latter course, and was coldly received by the majordomo, who doubted whether the notes had been paid by himself. As the sum was rather large, Herr Dicker became too persuasive, and was bundled out of the house. A few hours later, as he was brooding over the business apti- tudes required in dealings with Russians, he received the visit of a police inspector and two underlings, who wanted to know why he had not made a declaration at the police-office of having forged notes in his possession ? Herr Dicker ought now with alacrity to have ordered up a bottle of his best, and, while regaling the inspector, he should have slipped into his hands as many genuine notes as he could spare ; meantime Otto Dicker should have refreshed the underlings in another room, and have made little presents to them also. Then all would have gone well with the German household.

Unluckily, the German was in a bad temper, and began to talk nonsense about giving the Archimandrite's servant into custody. The inspec- tor, seeing no signs of coin, threw off the con- ciliatory attitude he had adopted upon entering, and announced that he was going to search the pre- mises. His two men, a pair of bullet-headed churls with grey coats and brass-hilted swords, thereupon went to work, and in less than an hour the German's house looked as if it had been ransacked by thieves.

Dicker was made—and not gently either—to open

every cupboard, desk, and box; his clothes, his wife's and daughter's, were strewn over the floors; the pockets of himself and family were turned inside out; finally the police went down to the cellars and set the barrel-cocks running to see whether these receptacles did really contain liquor, and not implements of forgery.

Herr Dicker imprudently stamped about, yelling imprecations in the dialect of Pomerania. He was exhorted to hold his peace. The police made up all his notes, money, and portable trinkets into a parcel with one of his own napkins, telling him that every article proved to be lawfully his would be restored to him. Then the inspector said sharply, 'Now come along.' 'Where to?' asked Herr Dicker, with his hair-roots stiffening. 'To prison,' answered the inspector; and off they all went, to the amusement of the people in the streets, who are always gratified at seeing a German in trouble.

A Russian gaol is not built on any wasteful plan of keeping prisoners warm and comfortable. A black, mouldy house situate in one of the slums of the town, it is guarded by a dozen crop-headed soldiers and has a painted 'scutcheon with the Imperial double-headed eagle over the gate. There is a whipping post in the front yard. Thieves, murderers, boys, lunatics, women are all huddled together in a room of foul stenches warmed by a stove, and the only food served out to them is a pound of black bread in the morning and a mess of rancid soup at midday. The sexes are separated at night.

By day the prisoners busy themselves as they can. Some are driven out in gangs to repair the roads or clear the snow from the streets ; others make shoes or sculpture wooden toys ; and others do nothing but snooze in corners, sleeping off the effects of the vodki which they have bribed the warders to buy. Acts of insubordination are punished by whipping, and the women get as much of this punishment as the men. It is no longer customary for judges to sentence prisoners to be flogged, but gaol governors are empowered to maintain discipline by stripes ; and thus a servant girl, who is committed for trial on a charge of thieving, often gets a smart flagellation or two at the hands of a stout-armed wardress by private arrangement between the governor and her mistress. In these gaols it is only well-to-do prisoners who are placed in solitary confinement.

Herr Dicker being well-to-do was thrust into a cell furnished with a bundle of straw and floored with damp flags. Water dripped from the walls and rats poked their noses out of holes, staring at him in the twilight. He had a piece of black

bread for supper, but remained from dusk to dawn
without lights, for no candles were allowed. All
this did not tame him, but made him gnash his teeth
and swear to be even with the Archimandrite's servant.
In the morning a hungry-looking gaoler hinted that
he could have a decent room and good food by paying
for them. Herr Dicker shouted that he would pay
nothing.

Shortly afterwards he was called into an upper
chamber to see an examining magistrate in a black
uniform with pewter buttons, who significantly told
him that justice was resolved to make an example
of those who uttered forged notes. Herr Dicker
looked as if he were going to have a fit; he was,
indeed, so blinded by wrath as not to notice that he
was alone with the magistrate, and could consequently
prove his innocence by the promise of a small cash
payment. The dignitary gave him every chance by
throwing out some feeling allusions to the discomforts
of being sent to work in the silver mines of Siberia;
but the dull German would take no hints, and it was
too late when the magistrate's clerk was summoned
in to copy down the prisoner's depositions. Then the
magistrate began browbeating as if he had got a confirmed rogue in his clutches. He abused Herr Dicker,
and asked him if he would confess. 'Confess what?'

asked the German. 'Oh, we'll bring you to your
senses,' cried the tightly-buttoned little gentleman;
and, as the hotel-keeper would do nothing but protest
his innocence, he was taken back to spend another
day with the rats.

Meanwhile Frau Dicker, a sagacious woman, be-
thought her that when a man falls into a pit or a
Russian prison, the first thing to do is to pull him out
without caring how he got there. Her husband's
hotel was much frequented by officers who came
thither to drink; and, among others, the lieutenant-
colonel, chief inspector of forage, owed a bill of 300
silver roubles for bottles of Rhenish wine. It grieved
the German housewife to receipt this account unpaid,.
but she bravely did so; and, moreover, put into a
basket six bottles of Liebfraumilch (which the inspector of forage loved); then, having donned her best
catskin cloak, she set out to see the colonel along with
her daughter Lisa, a personable damsel, who cried as
she went.

The honest colonel was touched by the tears,
the wine, and the receipted bill, and promised that
the mistake which had led to Herr Dicker's arrest
should be explained in the proper quarters. But it
turned out that the hotel-keeper was in perilous
plight; for the Archimandrite was much shocked that

his servant should have been accused of uttering
forged notes, while as to the servant himself, he declared that nothing would atone for the injury he had
suffered.

However, a plaster for the servant's wounded
feelings was found in the shape of a hundred-rouble
note; after which nothing remained but to plaster the
examining magistrate, the inspector of police (whose
plastering in the first instance would have saved all
this trouble), and the prison governor, who else might
have made a hubbub. This done, Herr Dicker was
released from gaol after a confinement of three days.
But sad it is to say that he behaved wrong-headedly
as soon as he got home; for, thinking that his libera-
tion was due to his own blamelessness, he flew into
the worst of rages with Frau Dicker for having behaved as if he had been guilty. The wives of innocent
men have often much to put up with.

One of the results of this little adventure was that
Herr Dicker looked very sharply at his bank-notes in
future. He nearly got into trouble a second time for
refusing a true note which he alleged to be false.
Then he had a disturbance with his wife's friend, the
forage colonel, for paying him a false note which was
traced up to the military paymaster, who had got it
from the Bank, whose manager took a long time to

convince himself that it was sham, and only exchanged it for a good one after much grumbling. It befell at this juncture that the Holy War against the Turks was declared, when an Imperial decree ordered all Russians to carry their bank-notes to the offices of the tax-receivers, who, by stamping them, took 5 per cent. off their value. The effect of this ingenious war-tax was to increase the circulation of false notes prodigiously, so that people soon ceased to trouble themselves whether they held good paper or bad.

But Herr Dicker troubled himself, because he owed a grudge to the Archimandrite's servant and wished to catch that worthy tripping. He had a keen eye for flash paper, and mentioned to some friends whom he knew to have dealings with the servant that if they could catch that person uttering a false note they should be rewarded for their trouble. This reached the servant's ears and made him uncomfortable, for he did not wish to put his good master to the expense of bribing him out of the scrape; so he prayed the Archimandrite to be careful about the notes he received, and that pious man became, in truth, so careful that all who came into contact with him caught the contagion.

Three or four suspicious men in a town can play havoc with a paper currency; and, owing to Herr

Dicker's grudge, business relations grew extremely difficult in K——. The Civil Governor, noting the general disaffection resulting from this and tracing the evil to its source, decided that if Herr Dicker could be put back into prison and kept there for a season the public weal would be enhanced.

It is not difficult to get an hotel-keeper into trouble. Herr Dicker was arrested for neglecting to make a passing stranger, who slept a night in his house, exhibit his passport, whereby, said the police, a person presumed to be a dangerous con- spirator had gone off, leaving no clue. Herr Dicker once under lock and key, the Archimandrite's servant ceased to vex himself about his bank-notes; so did the Archimandrite, the forage colonel, and many others; whence in an incredibly short space of time the flow of false notes and of mutual confidence was resumed, to the general satisfaction in the town of K——.

As for Frau Dicker, remembering how her hus- band had treated her, she avoided incurring his re- proach by bribing him out a second time, and managed the hotel by herself—not uncheerfully. Herr Dicker was released after three months, lean as a herring and sadly rheumatic. And he was an altered man in mind as well as body. The first time that a flash note was brought him he respectfully gave change for it in

other flash notes, doing in Russia as the Russians do;
and he took an early opportunity of resuming convivial relations with the Archimandrite's servant. Thus
the chastening of experience works for the good of
us all.

CHAPTER XI.

THE WHITE CLERGY.

THE 'white' clergy in Russia are the ordinary popes and deacons who hold cure of souls: the 'black' clergy are the monks, from whose ranks all the Church dignitaries are chosen.

Black and white detest one another with a cordiality not often seen in less pious countries. A man cannot become a white clergyman unless he is married; he cannot retain his benefice after his wife's death, and he must not marry a second time; so upon becoming a widower he relapses into civil life or turns monk. But as a monk he cannot aspire to dignities, for his marriage disqualifies him from becoming a bishop; he must possess his soul in patience, and see all the mitres given away to monks who have been single all their days.

Until recently a man was compelled to enter the Church, either as pope or monk, simply from the fact that he was a clergyman's son; nowadays, the bishop may release a young man from this obligation, but they are not bound to do so whenever applied to. They refuse if their dioceses be ill stocked with clergy ; and at best they will only allow a clergyman's son to enter the civil or military service of the Crown ; they will not permit him to become a tradesman.

A layman's son finds it easy to become a monk, for candidates to the black clergy are 'rare ; but if he wants to turn pope he must ' prove his vocation ' by paying a fair sum of money and furnishing numerous certificates of his own and his parents' morality ; but even then he will only be admitted if the diocese which he seeks to enter stands in need of recruits.

The white clergy form a close caste, and it has been the policy of the synods to maintain this state of things by strict laws as to clerical marriages. A candidate for orders must marry the widow, daughter, or sister of a pope, and his bishop often compels him to choose his bride within the diocese. A clergyman's widow or daughter who would like to marry a layman has to deny herself that pleasure unless her lover is prepared to pay a thousand roubles or so privately to the bishop to purchase her ; on the other hand, clerical families find an inducement to adhere to their order from the fact that benefices are hereditary. A son succeeds to his father almost as a matter of course ; and if a pope leaves only daughters, his benefice will be kept open for a reasonable time, till the eldest marries and brings it to her husband as a dower.

Popes have to pay lighting and paving rates (in places where there are lights and pavements), but they are exempted from all Government taxes, from military recruitment, and billeting. In cases of offence against the common law they cannot be sentenced to corporal punishment, nor in prison are their heads shaved ; and all these privileges and immunities extend to their wives and to the children born to them after ordination. However, a pope who commits some very disgraceful offence, or who incurs the wrath of Government—which comes to the same thing—can be unfrocked and drafted into the army, or be transported to Siberia, without any tedious formalities.

The white clergy accuse the black of diverting from them the benefactions of the faithful, and of misappropriating the Church revenues generally ; the black reply that the white are a set of dissolute fellows who have more than enough money as it is, and grow fat by roguery. The people, viewing with an equal

eye the merits of the two clergies, think there is little
to choose between them in the matter of peculation ;
but they despise the white clergy most because the
malpractices of the popes are more palpable. The
budget of the secular clergy amounts to £5,000,000,
which, distributed among 36,000 parishes, gives about
£140 to each. By rights there should be in each
parish a pope, a deacon, and two clerks, but there are
only 12,000 deacons and 60,000 clerks in the whole
empire ; consequently, as half the income of each
parish should go to the pope, every pope ought to
receive about £85 a year. He gets nothing like that,
for the bishops act as if the establishment of deacons
and clerks was complete, and put the surplus salaries
into their pockets. The synods also rob him, and at
times (for instance, during the war) neglect to pay
him at all.

The pope therefore swindles for a living. But
one need not pity him overmuch, for the sums which
he makes by his extortions more than counter-
balance the salary of which he is defrauded. In the
towns the popes live high ; in the villages their homes
are always comfortable. As we mentioned in a former
chapter, the popes are generally agents for the sale of
vodki ; and in addition to this they make money by
the Easter gifts of the rich, by subscriptions raised

among the poor to buy church images (from which they always deduct a good percentage), by requiring fees for baptisms, burials, weddings, &c., by signing eucharistical certificates and certificates of character, by intimidating and ransoming dissenters, and by wringing death-bed donations out of the sick, which they often do with impious menaces.

A Russian priest will do nothing for you without payment, and there are few things he will not do if well paid. He will accept a kopeck sooner than nothing, but he takes care to get a rouble out of you if he thinks you can afford it. The loathing felt for the white clergy by rich as well as poor would drive millions of Russians into overt Nihilism, if it were not for the fearful penalties to which persons are liable when they desert the Orthodox faith in which they have been bred.

A Russian who is born a Jew, Catholic, or Raskolnik (dissenter) may live in his heresy, subject to certain restrictions in the exercise of his religion and to numerous civil and social disabilities. But a man born in the Orthodox faith may be transported to Siberia if he publicly abjures it. And transported he will be, unless he compounds with the parish priest according to his means. Dissent is therefore a source of revenue to the established clergy, and they wink at it to such an extent that there are more than two hundred heretical sects flourishing among the nominally Orthodox Russians. The Church of the Holy Empire is, in fact, cankered and honeycombed with infidelity. Every form of craziness, grotesqueness, sanguinary wildness and obscenity is embraced in the tenets of the heretical sects ; and all the members of them who want to be left alone pay black-mail. They cannot avoid doing so, for the law obliges every Orthodox Russian to provide himself with an eucharistical certificate, setting forth that he has duly shriven himself and partaken of the Communion at Easter.

On these eucharistical certificates, which can always be bought for a fee, is based the pompous report which the Procurator of the State Synod addresses yearly to the Czar on the subject of religion in the empire. This functionary makes no allusion to dissent, and he gravely writes of the clergy that they ' set a shining example of all the Christian virtues.' Nevertheless he lets slip some admissions which read oddly. Thus, according to the last report published, it is in the army that religious duties are most zealously performed—this military zeal being a matter of compulsion. Next in order of piety come the peasants, then the Civil Servants of the Crown, then the publicans, and lastly, polite society. The commercial classes are nowhere ; and there are 25 per cent. of the supposed Orthodox Russians who do not show up eucharistical certificates at all.

How comes there to be such an immense number of persons who defy the law ? The thing would be inexplicable but for the corruptness of the priests in making capital out of dissent, and for a peculiar fanatical twist in Russian character which will impel a man who has bought an eucharistical certificate out of prudence to tear it up, stamp and spit upon it afterwards, to vent his spite against the priest who sold it to him. Or, again, a heretic will bribe a priest to let him alone, but will decline to take out a certificate lest it should defile him ; in either case the pope shrugs his shoulders and has no interest in proceeding against the man, nor will anybody else proceed against him if the pope does not.

One can understand after this how it comes that in popular songs the pope, his wife, and clerk should appear as butts for the most savage satire ; but the peasants who laugh loudest against the priest will be foremost in prostrating themselves inside the churches. The Russians sever the Church and the clergy altogether, and the foulest dissenting sects go to the places of worship. As for the popes, loose fish as they

are, they are not sceptics. They believe in the bodily
presence of the Evil One, so much so that they are
afraid of meeting him after dark. They howl during
thunderstorms ; they bang their heads against the
altar steps when they have dipped in some unusual
piece of roguery ; and they have a queer theology of
their own by which they hope to be saved if they stick
faithfully to rubrics.

A Russian priest will seriously tell you that
it is allowable to get drunk but not to smoke,
because ' not that which goeth in but that which
cometh out of the mouth defileth a man ;' and he
will argue that the saying ' a priest must live by the
altar ' means that he should make the altar yield all
it can—that it is a talent confided to him, and that he
would be a slothful servant if he hid it in a napkin.
But it is in devising salves for the consciences of rich
penitents that the Russian clergy shine most. One
of them, desirous of soothing a wealthy barina, informed her that it is not good to be faultless ; for
perfect virtue is apt to beget pride, which is a deadly
sin, and consequently quite as grievous a matter as
the particular sin of which the lady in question had
accused herself. The author of this comforting axiom
in morals was, however, not a humble pope, but a
bishop ; as doubtless he deserved to be.

CHAPTER XII.

THE DAIMONIKS OF EKATERINOSLAV.

ONE of the prettiest towns of Southern Russia is Ekaterinoslav, founded by Catherine II. under circumstances strongly suggestive of the manner in which things were done in the Empire a hundred years ago, as now.

Potemkin, having conquered the vast district at present called New Russia, prevailed upon the Empress, whose favourite he was, to come and visit it in state ; but there was nothing for her Majesty to see beyond steppes covered with vultures and avrotchkis (corn-eating rats), so the general gallantly extemporized a series of sham villages all along the Imperial route. Wherever the Empress stopped she was regaled with the sight of brightly painted cottages and peasantry in holiday attire, who yelled hymns in her honour. Delighted with all she saw, the kind-hearted Empress instituted serfdom among her new subjects, and, coming to a picturesque spot on the

Dnieper, with hills, birch trees, and so forth, decided she would there found a city which should be the St. Petersburg of the south.

This programme has not yet been fulfilled; but there is no guessing the possibilities of a town which stands in the middle of an immense tract of coal-mines, and whose river may become navigable some day when Russians may go to work without having the Tschinn to reckon with. Meantime Ekaterinoslav has a showy boulevard, a mineralogical museum (formerly the palace of Potemkin, who was presented by his mistress with a million acres of land in the neighbourhood), a French hotel with beds, which are unusual luxuries in Russian hostelries, and a number of half-built palaces, in which the nobility of the district come to lodge at the triennial assemblies of nobles.

The inhabitants of Ekaterinoslav not being much occupied in overreaching one another in commerce, and the Civil servants finding time hang heavy on their hands, there is a great deal of leisure for the cultivation of small talk and metaphysics; and, in fact, the town plumes itself on being one of the centres of Russian thought. The ladies dress in the Parisian fashions of the year before last and babble a sort of French derived from the novels of M. Paul de Kock. Many of the shops affect French sign-boards, and the place seems to have attractions for Gascon barbers and cooks, who having failed in business on the banks of the Garonne, come here to quarrel with square-headed Germans who sell musical instruments and teach arithmetic in the schools.

In Ekaterinoslav, as elsewhere, the 'thought' of society is disloyal; for whenever Russians fall to thinking they think ill of their rulers. Ladies who receive you to tea chatter about constitutionalism, the immorality of the priesthood, and the latest fads in political economy, as if these refreshing topics were the best things to promote conviviality. Men are equally babblesome with the frondeur spirit, and, provided neither the civil nor military governor be present to act as wet blanket, will talk of an impending revolution as of a coming family dance in which all good Russians will be delighted to join. For a long time strangers mistook these signs for the mere magpie garrulousness of people who were bored and wanted to show off before foreigners as intellectual beings; but the prestige of the Romanoff dynasty is chiefly based on the supposition of the Czar's invincible military might and would not bear the stress of defeat. For the sake of invincibility—for the sake of maintaining that mammoth army of four million men, on paper, which is believed to make Europe tremble— the Russian would put up with a great deal ; but, let the Czar be once well beaten, his flag disgraced and Russian credit destroyed, then it would be seen that the national discontent is no superficial thing.

In Ekaterinoslav there are several hundred Raskolniks, who walk about with the flowing beards and long robes of the Old Russians, and protest against the depravity of their contemporaries by a style of living austerely Puritan ; there are Nihilists, and Steouriks, and Bejemschiks, whose gods are Voltaire, Stenko-Razin, and Pougatcheff (the revolutionary Socialists) ; there are Daimoniks, whose worship resembles adoration of the Evil One ; there are Mirskites, or members of country mirs, who, being allowed to work as servants or workmen in the towns, have to pay their communes more than half their earnings and grumble at this obligation with a ferocious sullenness ; and there is an official journal, which comes out twice a week, printed on grey candle-paper, and takes no more heed of these excited sects and factions than if they were cutting their capers in China.

Latterly, however, the candle-paper journal did

have to notice the strange goings-on of a Countess
Olga Nervski, who, at a time when the authorities
had their hands full with raising recruits for the war,
suddenly threw the town into convulsions by espous-
ing the tenets of the Daimoniks just mentioned.
One Sunday the Countess, who is a widow, began
shrieking in church at the top of her contralto voice.
The pope stopped in the middle of his prayers ;
the sacristans bustled forward to her assistance ; but
it was soon seen that the Countess was not labouring
under a mere fit of hysterics, but intended to go on
shrieking until others joined her. The church was
soon filled with howling, for a Russian has only to
give tongue for another to chime in without caring
why ; and so the congregation broke up in disorder.
Then the Countess, tearing off her French bonnet and
letting her hair flow down her back, rushed out of
church, followed by a sympathetic crowd, among
whom the driver of her droschki tried to plough his
way, thwacking his horses and shedding tears of ex-
citement.

It was soon known that Olga Marienvna, as
her intimates called her, had been 'illuminated ; '
but with what sort of a light only appeared in the
evening when, amidst a circle of guests who were
drinking punch *à la Grassot* and tea flavoured with

lemon-juice, she announced that she would die in the faith of the Daimoniks. The faith in question proceeds from the assumption that as the Evil One has the largest share in the government of this world, and of Russia in particular, insomuch that there is no avoiding his decrees, the best way to act is to try and make friends with him by throwing aside all moral restraints whatsoever. The Daimoniks trust that Diabolos, being touched, will refuse to admit into any place of torment the soul that served him so well. Nay, that the very weakness which induced the soul to rely on Diabolos may be accepted as a plea for mercy in the courts above ; or that in any case the soul, being refused above and below, will float about in space enjoying eternal sleep.

If the Countess Olga had lived in the Emperor Nicholas's time she would not have joined these Daimoniks, for the civil governor would have had her taken to the police-office and privately whipped ; but the present Czar has never understood his father's policy of treating Russians like schoolboys and school-girls, though, on the other hand, he has failed to see that in raising his subjects to the dignity of grown-up persons he should have given them employment fit for adults.

The natural result of the half-and-half policy has

been that educated Russians like the Countess and her friends—finding no scope for their independent energies, and being nevertheless continually inflamed by the liberal literature of the West, which comes pouring over the frontier like so much lava—are liable to grow crazy. After expounding her faith hysterically for a couple of days in her own home, to the conversion of her attached domestics and dinner-table hangers-on, the Countess one morning vanished into the country and began to scatter the doctrines of her new faith among the peasantry.

It is not rare in Russia to meet with hallucinated ladies devoting themselves to missions of this sort ; and had there been no war going on the Countess Olga might have been left to compound her heresy by payments to the clergy, and afterwards go her ways until her demoniacal fever spent itself, which would doubtless have been soon.

But in times when the popular nerves are strained to the tightest tension-point religious outbreaks may become the rallying-points for political disturbances ; wherefore the authorities of Ekaterinoslav grew uneasy. For some time past the humour of the townsfolk had been sulky and obstreperous, for this was at the outset of the campaign while the Turks were getting the best of it. The little candle-paper journal, after

telling untruths about the war with surprising effrontery, had been at last compelled to own that things
were not going on as they ought ; private letters from
the Danube told the same story ; and in fact the pro-
pagation by a rich and comely widow of a heresy
which flaunted defiance at everything and everybody
was just likely to commend itself to the mood of a
population sick to death of showing respect to their
betters.

So a batch of policemen were sent in quest of
the Countess Olga, and she was brought back ; but
the Civil Governor, being a gentleman and coated over
with a French polish of scepticism and urbanity,
thought it better to reason laughingly with the lady
than to punish her ; and this device succeeded. Olga
Marienvna ended by laughing too, and went back to
her house saying that her illumination (in which,
mayhap, she had seen a vision of Siberian snows) had
passed away. But it did not pass away from the
minds of others, whose brains she had set on fire, and
it must have caused Olga Marienvna a thrill of horror
to hear that the police and the military were going
about apprehending all the low-class Daimoniks, with
a number of Nihilists and Bejemschiks into the bargain, and enrolling them by force into the army.

This is the usual upshot of such affairs. The

Russian army must have soldiers ; and, as the peasantry hide away like field mice from the search of the recruiting officers in times of disaster, a conspiracy or a riot comes as a welcome pretext for impressment. The Daimonik business saved the Governor of Ekaterinoslav the trouble of resorting to the expedient adopted by his colleague at Novgorod, who pounced upon all the able-bodied buyers and sellers who had come to the annual fair. It also purged his town for a while of discontented spirits, and gave the little candle-paper journal an opportunity of writing that the pressed men had all enlisted voluntarily, and 'had, indeed, gone away anxious to atone for a passing aberration by loyal service to their country thenceforth.' That is the way they manage official journalism in Holy Russia.

CHAPTER XIII.

A BOOKSELLER AND PUBLISHER.

OVER the front of a shop painted bright yellow in the Czarina Prospect of Ekaterinoslav are these words in Russo-French : 'Triknieff — Libraire et Publieur.' Triknieff has been told a hundred times that the French for publisher is *éditeur* ; but a Russian takes tender liberties with the languages he loves—as witness that barber lower down the street, who, to cut out a French rival over the way, goes in for Anglicism with the announcement : 'Ruzski ; Inglish Shaver.'

Triknieff, though, is not an ignorant man, for he holds a mart for the works of human intellect published all the world over. His shop is full of French, English, and German books. He publishes works in the Russian tongue, he owns a monthly magazine, and would have started a weekly newspaper before now if the town where he flourishes had possessed that inestimable boon, a censor. Scores of Russian towns are crying out for censors, but there are only nine censorial commissions in the whole empire, and every book or magazine essay which Triknieff wishes to put forth must be sent to Odessa for approval.

Three months is the shortest time that can elapse before he gets back his manuscript, more or less embellished with corrections in red pencil ; but sometimes six months slip by, for the censors have a great deal to do. If a work contains strictures upon anything connected whith Government service it must be referred to the State department in St. Petersburg which those strictures concern ; and this often involves a delay of years. For these reasons Triknieff has to get his magazine made up months beforehand ; but even then he is not sure of being able to sell it ; for an essay which was innocuous at the time when it received the imprimatur may, through a turn in circumstances, become perilous reading, in which case the magazine is seized. Last year Triknieff received a well-written work upon the difficulties of a campaign on the Danube ; but as these difficulties regarded the War Office, the book was forwarded thither, and there it is lying now. Perhaps Triknieff will be allowed to publish it, with amendments, towards the beginning of 1879, if he should think the subject still retains interest then.

Triknieff would be a happy man if Government

would instal a censor in his town and arm him with full powers ; but he and Government look at this question from opposite points of view ; for Triknieff wants to promote the sale of literature and Government desires to check it. It is more than enough for the authorities that publications should come out with tolerable frequency in the nine university towns—St. Petersburg, Moscow, Kazan, Dorpat, Vilna (Lithuania), Kiev, Kharkov, Odessa, and Warsaw. All these places possess censors, and most of them one or two daily independent newspapers, whose articles have to be submitted for revision three clear days before going to print ; but, if country-town censors were appointed, Triknieff and his fellows would soon get bribing them, and there would be no damming up the torrent of prints that would well up, to the flooding of institutions that could no longer stand if the waters of publicity were let into them.

These things have been benevolently explained to Triknieff by the civil governor more than once, and the shrewd old gentleman has advised the publisher to be content with such wit as he has for cheating the censorship as often as he can. Triknieff understands what this means, for he is only trammelled by the censors so far as outward appearances go. What these gentlemen virtually

I

do is to hinder his publication of works by respectable native writers and to mutilate foreign works
forwarded to him by his agent at Leipzic ; but
in the matter of issuing anonymous Socialist pam-
phlets, or boudoir romances such as could not
be suffered to lie on any decent boudoir table,
Triknieff, like the rest of his craft in Russia, is free.

He has a clandestine press and numerous secret
hawkers who help him to disseminate tons of foolish
and foul literature, with the tacit connivance of the
police, whom he suborns.   If you asked him for Mill's
' Political Economy ' over his counter, he would tell
you that the work is forbidden ; if you wanted to buy
Thackeray's ' Virginians ' you would find about five
dozen pages cut out.   The works of Voltaire, Thiers,
Macaulay, and Victor Hugo are not to be seen on
Triknieff's shelves ; those of Dickens, Balzac, and the
elder Dumas are only purchasable (publicly) in an
incomplete form ; but, if the honest bookseller has to
deal with a man of position or with a lady whom he
can trust, he will come after dark, bringing a cargo
not only of the works asked for, but of numerous
others of which it would not be expedient so much as
to utter the names aloud.

The Russians are great readers, and the difficulty of procuring good foreign works in open

day makes every one privy, more or less, to the malpractices of booksellers. Long before the censors have made up their minds as to M. Victor Hugo's last production, ' The History of a Crime,' the work will have been read by every Russian who cares to pay the high price for which smuggled or pirated copies can be bought. But extravagant prices are naturally a bar to persons of moderate means ; and that is how it comes that the pomeschiks, or small squires, the trading classes, university students, and subaltern officers have exhausted the frivolous in literature ; and when they have exhausted the frivolous then hawkers tempt their jaded appetites, as above said, with licentious books under alluring titles.

Much of the corruption of women in Russian society —corruption which often finds vent in hysteric outbreaks towards Nihilism, Daimonism, or what not—comes of the fearful books that are devoured for want of better mental food. The Russian bookseller is, in fact, a wholesale polluter of morals; and yet such a one as Triknieff, in the Czarina Prospect, only trades in vice because he would have to shut up shop if he confined himself to the lawful sale of books allowed by the censors. Give him freedom of bookselling, and he would be the first to suppress the clandestine branch of his trade, being a respectable man often to be seen in church along with his wife—who, it is to be hoped, knows nothing of the strange works piled up in his cellars.

Triknieff's expenses are high, for he keeps three founts of type—Russian, German, and French—and has a staff of compositors who can print in three languages. Skilled labour is always dear in Russia, and the artels of printers have latterly forced up the wages of their hands to three paper roubles a day. It needs a sale of many books to cover such prices ; but when it is considered that Triknieff keeps about half a dozen police officials in hush-money, and has to pay two or three yearly visits to Odessa to propitiate censors and get whole boxes of foreign books through the custom-house uninspected, the only wonder is that he can make the two ends meet at all. His shop is almost always empty, and he gives away so many gratis copies of his uninteresting magazine that its selling circulation can hardly meet the cost of printing.

Probably he keeps up this periodical for the respectability it gives him. He is an honorary member of several provincial academies ; an inspector of schools (which confers on him the right to a bright blue uniform and a star with three points) ; he sits in the municipal council of his town and on the jury at assizes ; and he is generally regarded as a first-class savant. His magazine treats of science and agriculture; publishes adaptations of French and English sensation novels; and is of course profoundly and gushingly loyal. The contributors are generally amateurs in the service of the Crown who like to see themselves in print; but there is a sub-editor, a polyglot Pole, who pads the pages with translations from foreign periodicals when original matter fails.

Triknieff is great at piracies, and when a foreign novel is passed by the censors and seems likely to have a good sale, he will reprint it sooner than go to the expense of ordering copies from abroad. Some of these reprints read oddly, for, with a view to economy, all that is not 'action' in the book—disquisitions, descriptions of scenery, &c.—are expunged. The polyglot Pole has a marked talent for compressing three volumes into one, and will often give a work the touch of literary finish, either by an addition of sensationalism or by a readjustment of 'scenes,' which in his opinion it lacks. More often, however, the works which Triknieff pirates are those which the censors have banned; and then the Pole is useful for dressing up these books in Russian garb, denationalizing the characters and their names.

Triknieff prints more things in Russian than in French or German; though works in these last two

languages always command a sale among those who
aspire at gentility. His magazine is Russian, and
as such is viewed with favour by the authorities,
who like to be able to show by palpable proof how
the Czar's Government encourages native literature.
It is probable, indeed, that if from some cause or other
Triknieff was compelled to abandon the publication
of his periodical, somebody else would be assisted to
bring it out, so that it might not be said that gravely
instructive literature had ceased to be in demand in
any of his Majesty's provinces.   As it is, the magazine
undoubtedly does Triknieff a good turn by giving him
the decent name which he could hardly derive from
his other literary transactions.   It is like the reputable
flag which a pirate hoists when he sails with a cargo
of contraband.

CHAPTER XIV.

NEWSPAPERS AND REVIEWS.

IT would be unfair to class all Russian reviews along with the magazine published by Triknieff, of Ekater-isnoslav. St. Petersburg and Moscow have some excellent reviews, a few well-written daily papers, and half-a-dozen comic journals that are really funny and very licentious. Among these last the *Svistok* ('Whistle') and the *Iskra* ('Spark') deserve an honourable mention, both for their letterpress and caricatures. Their artists are trained in the French school, but go further than Parisian cartoonists would dare to do. They valiantly attack all but the strong —the smaller tyrants of the bureaucracy, private persons, monks, ladies, foreigners ; and nobody has any remedy against them, for they are protected by powerful persons whom these attacks amuse.

Some years ago a facetiously abominable little print, called the *Veseltchak* ('Wag'), was suppressed for a series of bitter lampoons on the private life of a

foreign Sovereign ; but it was no secret that these
attacks had been inspired by a high official not uncon-
nected with the Ministry of Police ; and the editor
forthwith reissued his paper under a new name, the
Goudok, thereby proving that he had sufficient interest
in official quarters, for otherwise he could not have
obtained the necessary licence. A Russian newspaper proprietor must first obtain permission to print,
then lodge 2,500 silver roubles as caution money ;
after which he becomes subject to a régime of ' admonitions,' two of which entail a suspension for a term of
two months. Those who cannot afford to lodge
caution money—which they are not likely ever to
see again, for it is forfeited in case the paper
is suppressed—have to submit to a preventive
censorship by sending their articles to the censors
three clear days beforehand.

In provincial towns where there are no censors,
and where a man does not care to throw away
£400, journalism is non-existent ; but even in the
two capitals, and in such large cities as Kiev and
Odessa, a proprietor who has paid caution money
finds it prudent to let the censors have a peep
at the articles he is going to print—or, at least, he
submits them to one or other of the great people
whom every Russian newspaper has behind it. Inde-

pendent journalism, as understood in other countries, does not exist in Russia. If a man were guilelessly to suppose that because he had fulfilled the legal formalities he could carry on a newspaper without official support, it would not take him a week to discover his mistake, for all the profits of his circulation would be swallowed up in compounding with tschinovniks, who would threaten him with admonitions and lawsuits.

There are at this moment 475 daily, weekly, or bi-weekly journals in Russia, 377 of them being published in the native tongue. Of this total 36 papers are the property of universities and colleges, 161 belong to trade guilds or professional artels, 101 are official journals published under the direction of provincial governors, and the remainder are all in the hands of influential magnates, who employ them more to gratify private malice or ambition than to serve public ends.

The most eminent of so-called independent papers in the capital, the *Golos* ('Voice'), is the organ of the Czar's intimate friends, the Bariatinskis, and the liberalism it affects has its source at Court. The *Journal de St. Pétersbourg*, edited by a Belgian, and published in French, is the pet paper of Chancellor Gortschakoff and his friends. The *Invalide* is sup-

ported by the War Office and is the mouthpiece of
the old Russian Chauvin party, while its rival, the
Russian World, edited by General Fadeieff, a clever
man, advocates military reforms under the ægis of the
Czarewitch. The *St. Petersburg News*, also called
the *Academical Gazette*, was recently purchased of the
Academy by the Ministry of Public Instruction, and
has no definite policy, but goes in for personalities
against all who make themselves disagreeable to
official authors, artists, doctors, and the ladies of the
Imperial operas. It was this journal that clamoured
for the recall of the Russian female students at Zurich,
and egged on the prosecution which has resulted in
the transportation of several of these poor girls to
Siberia. Among the best known provincial papers
the *Odessa Messenger*, whose literary articles are remarkable, belongs to the Lycée Richelieu; the
Kievlanine of Kiev is the property of monks; finally,
there is the *Moscow Gazette*, edited by M. Katkoff,
which for brilliancy and fearless hard-hitting excels
the other papers in the Empire.

This journal belongs to the University of Moscow,
but M. Katkoff has lately hired it on lease for twelve
years in consideration of a yearly payment of 74,000
silver roubles (£11,840). This is a great rental, but
the circulation of the paper exceeds 40,000 copies

a day, and it has a monopoly of the advertisements
in Moscow. M. Katkoff is the most eminent journalist in Russia, and, being a friend of the Czar,
as well as the pet of the Panslavist party, wields
unquestionable power, though not so much as he
did ten years ago. In 1866 he had influence enough
to overthrow M. Valouïef, Minister of the Interior,
who had presumed to suspend his journal, and
he caused M. Milutine to be set up in his stead.
Since then he and M. Milutine have grown cool
towards each other ; for M. Katkoff is not the man to
go in leading-strings, and lashes out now and then
against official abuses in a style which does not dis-
please the Czar, but which cannot commend itself to
placemen.

M. Katkoff was originally a fervent advocate of
British Constitutionalism ; the Polish insurrection
changed his ideas, and now there is not a Russian who
hates England politically more than he. But he
speaks English faultlessly ; and his fancy for British
literature appears to have survived his love of other
things English, for a review which he conducts together with the *Moscow Gazette* is almost entirely
devoted to the reproduction of English novels and to
the criticism of works published in London.

This review, the *Russian Messenger*, is one of four

periodicals which occupy a foremost place in the literature of the Empire.   The others are the *European Messenger*, published in St. Petersburg, and dealing chiefly
with French works ; the *Annals of the Country*, and
the *Diëlo* ('Work ').   M. Katkoff's erudite reviewers
have a strong conservative bias : the essayists in the
other three magazines are more or less lively and
liberal.   Russian society looks forward to the first of
each month, when these reviews appear, with keen
interest, for under cover of literary criticism the
essayists deal unsparingly in political and social satire.
Most of them are men of great culture, and carry to
a high point of perfection that art of innuendo which
has always to be cultivated under despotic govern-
ments.   However, Government allows a much greater
latitude to reviewers than to journalists ; and much
more licence to writers in the two capitals generally
than to those in the provinces.   Many a literary essay
is published in the *Diëlo* which, if cut up into leaders
and printed at Kharkov, would send its writer to
prison.

The *Diëlo* is very fond of dallying with Nihilism,
and takes the works of Renan, Strauss, and Darwin
as texts for veritable sermons on infidelity—most
delightful for Russian ladies to read between two

cups of tea flavoured with rum. Most well-to-do
people subscribe to all four of the reviews : and,
besides finding therein the intellectual feast of satire
and atheism just mentioned, get a monthly supply of
serial stories by the most popular Russian novelists
—Ivan Tourguenieff, Dostoïevski, Tolstoï, Salhias,
Averkief, and others.

Many English readers are acquainted with the
romances of Ivan Tourguenieff, the author of ' Smoke,'
who could hold his own against any Western novelist ;
but those of Tolstoï and Dostoïevski are little known
outside Russia, although they would well deserve
translation.   As much cannot be said as to the works
of Averkief, Salhias, Avsienko, and Markévitch, who
are the inaugurators of the Russian ' new school,'
which calls itself realistic, but is a compound of extravagance and sensualism.   The gods of this new
school are evidently MM. Gustave Flaubert and Emile
Zola ; but, while striving to imitate the defects of
these Frenchmen, the Russian realists delight to copy
the mannerisms of M. Victor Hugo's latter-day method
in prose, which is hardly suited to the minute por-
trayal of social turpitudes.   Immorality described in
pompous language and with far-fetched metaphors
has a queer effect upon the Western reader ; but

Russian ladies and gentlemen are swearing at present by the works of Averkief and Salhias, whom they affect to rank above Tourguenieff, and so it must be presumed that these gifted writers hold up mirrors in which the society of the Holy Empire sees itself faithfully reflected.

CHAPTER XV.

MARRIAGE CUSTOMS.

RUSSIAN marriages are generally arranged through priests. Being matters of business, it is desirable that there should be no mistake as to the amount of dower which the bride is to bring, and there would very likely be mistakes if some member of the upper clergy were not to act as an intermediary in preparing the settlements. An archimandrite does much of the work that falls to notaries in other countries; only he charges more, and a portion of the dower is apt to stick between his fingers. A well-bred bridegroom must present a gift to a monastery and another to his parish church; the bride, through her friends, is expected to clothe some statue of a Virgin with a gown of silver brocade, enriched with more or less jewels according to the piety of the donor; and in some parts of Southern Russia she adds a gift of two white doves to the pope, which looks rather like a relic of the worship of Venus. The consent of parents is necessary for a marriage : until the age of thirty in the case of men, twenty-five in that of women ; but young people are at liberty to appeal to the civil authorities if consent be arbitrarily withheld. In this event the parents are called upon to show reason for their refusal. The reason must not be mercenary unless one of the young people be heir to a landed estate ; then the question is referred to the marshal of the nobility in the district, whose decisions are based upon expediency rather than upon fixed principles.

These appeals are rare, because the Russians are a marrying people and dispose of their children early. In the middle and lower classes men marry at twenty when not drafted by the conscription; in the higher aristocracy a young man goes the 'grand tour' before settling down, but he is often betrothed before starting to a young lady not yet out of the schoolroom, and he weds her immediately upon his return. There is no country which has so few old maids as Russia. The great ridicule attached to the title, when not borne by a nun, has possibly something to do with the unwillingness of ladies to sport it. When a girl has reached the age of twenty-five without finding a mate, she generally sets out on what she calls a pilgrimage if poor—on a round of travels if rich ; and in either case she turns up some years after as a widow. Widows are as plentiful as old spinsters are scarce ; and widows whose husbands were never seen are more numerous than the rest. Etiquette forbids any allusion to a lady's dead husband in her presence ; and this is, perhaps, sometimes convenient.

When a couple are engaged, a betrothal feast is held, and the bride elect has a lock of her hair cut off in the presence of witnesses, and given to the bridegroom, who in return presents a silver ring set with a turquoise, an almond cake, and a gift of bread and salt. From this moment the two are plighted ; nor can the relatives break the match except with the consent of the parties themselves, which is signified by a return of the ring and lock of hair. So much importance is attached to the ring, at least in the north of Russia, that among poor people who cannot afford silver and a turquoise, tin and a bit of blue stone are substituted. These betrothal rings are kept as heirlooms, but must not be made to serve twice—a son cannot give his bride the ring which his mother received, for instance ; though why this should be so is a mystery which the clergy, who sell the rings, could best explain.

On the wedding day the bride comes to church

dressed in white ; but it is only among the highest
classes, who copy Western fashions, that the bridal
costume is entirely white, and that a wreath of
orange-flower blossoms is used. Among Russians
pure light blue is the nuptial colour, and a coronet
of silver ribbon stands in place of the wreath. The
wedding-ring for the bride is of gold or some yellow
metal, but not a plain hoop ; it is generally a double
ring with enchased stars. The bridegroom has a ring,
too, which the bride puts on his finger in the presence
of the Pope after she has received his, and this is
mostly a plain one. The clergy make much ado
about the rings being of pure metal, and thereby
keep the sale of them in their hands, though it would
not always be safe to test the purity of the ecclesiastical gold with a touchstone. After the wedding
service, which comprises in some of the less civilized
districts the breaking of an earthenware vessel in
token that the bride renounces her own possession
(or is ready to smash all her father's crockery for
her husband's sake—explanations differ)—after this
there is an adjournment to a banquet in which
mulled *kvass* (small beer) and almond cakes play a
great part.

Weddings need not be celebrated before midday,
nor must they take place in a church. In fashionable

circles it is the custom to solemnize them in a drawing-room, and by candlelight. There is no departure on a honeymoon tour. The banquet is followed by a ball, then by a supper; and at this last repast, when held in houses where old customs are observed, a new satin slipper, supposed to be the bride's, is produced, and used as a drinking vessel by the bridegroom's friends, who pass it round and drink the bride's health in it till it is soaked through and will hold liquor no longer. In houses where speeches are made it is not the bridegroom, but the bride's father, who returns thanks when her health is drunk—this usage being owing to the fact that a father still retains authority over his child after she is married. He may summon her from her home to tend him when he is sick. If he lose his wife he may claim his married daughter's services as a housekeeper during the first three months of his widowhood: and he very often does so. If the daughter's husband die, her father may order her to return to his roof, and he becomes *de jure* the guardian of her children. None of these privileges is retained by a married woman's mother.

Divorces are not properly allowed in Russia, but a marriage can be annulled for informality; and so divorces are pretty frequent. It is only a question of money, like most Russian things. In Lithuania and some parts of Little Russia it is the custom for the bride's nearest relative to give her a slap on the face at the moment of leading her to the priest, the object of this being to establish, in case of need, that the bride married under compulsion—which would be enough to break the marriage. Russians themselves assure strangers that the slap is only a reminder to the bride to behave well in future ; but the true sense of it is that just stated, for otherwise the reminder would presumably be given by the bridegroom.

In some parts of the Empire the date of the marriage is left blank on the certificate ; and this again furnishes grounds for a divorce. In the Chersonese the pope intentionally omits to register the ages of the parties ; but there is no real need for any of these precautions, for the marriage laws are so complex that two parties willing to pay for the luxury of a separation can easily ferret out an ukase whose prescriptions were not scrupulously observed at their nuptials. It is the clergy who declare a marriage null, and they will connive at any trick for this purpose. It is not by any means rare for a lady of fickle affections to get her new lover to pay her husband a sum of money that he may consent to a divorce ; and this has been done even in social circles where a regard for decencies might have been

·expected. About a dozen years ago an Imperial decree was launched forbidding servants of the Crown below the fifth rank to apply for annulments of marriage except with the permission of their chiefs, which would have been absurd if such annulments had only been asked for, as a rule, upon sufficient grounds. Annulled ladies, whether remarried or not, are received into society ; so are those who have annulled marriages two or three times ; and, indeed, Russian morals as to the sanctity of marriage are nothing if not lax.

Russians make good husbands, according to their own ideas of good—that is, they are indulgent, good tempered, and not jealous ; but in the higher classes they are incorrigible flirts, and in the lower they drink, and, being drunk, settle all connubial differences by blows. It is a common sight in a village to see a mujick cuffing his wife with might and main ; nor do her howls bring any of her own sex to her assistance. It seems to be admitted among all but the upper classes that a man has full right to beat his wife, and she gets no sympathy whether she vociferates or hits back. In case of flagrant infidelity a Russian may have his wife put in prison for a year, and if she be not of noble blood or of a priest's family, he may have her once flogged besides ; but this prerogative is more honoured in the breach than in the observance. Women have no counter-hold over their husbands, and herein appears the Oriental view still prevailing in the Empire as to the ascendency of the strong sex. A husband may appear as a witness in a lawsuit against his wife, but a wife is not heard against her husband ; a man may oblige his wife to work for him, but a wife cannot sue her husband even for necessaries, and she has no redress against him if he deserts her.

Orientalism appears again in the almost total seclusion of Russian middle-rank women within their own homes. You must have known a Russian of the trading class for some time before he thinks it advisable to introduce his wife ; and you must have been his intimate friend for years before he would take the liberty of letting her sit down to table in your presence. Russian women go out of doors with their children, but seldom with their husbands ; and a man is not expected to take notice of another man's wife by bowing to her if she passes him in the streets. One of the sights which surprises a Russian of the midland cities most when he goes to St. Petersburg, Moscow, or Odessa is to notice the promiscuous flow of both sexes in the streets and in places of amusement. As to the spectacle of married ladies sitting in the boxes of theatres with their shoulders bare, this amazing licence is enough to take his breath away.

In writing of marriage customs one must not forget the marriage fairs, which are still held in some provincial towns during Easter week. It was formerly the practice, even in Moscow and St. Petersburg, for all the marriageable men and maidens to resort to the public gardens on Easter Sunday, and return there every day of the week. Rich men could take their pick. When a pretty face pleased them they addressed its owner directly, and asked the names of her parents. If open to an offer she gave the required information, and negotiations were commenced without delay. Country people used to travel from afar to attend these marriage fairs, which were not unlike the statute hirings in English markets, only that the damsels were hired for life ; but nowadays girls of the better classes have gradually abandoned the old custom, and in places where the fairs still exist they are chiefly frequented by servant girls. In some towns they have degenerated into saturnalia. Housemaids, who ask leave to attend them, stay away a week, and return at the end of that time unmarried often, and much the worse, physically and morally, for their seven days' carousing.

CHAPTER XVI.

MONKS AND NUNS.

WRITING of Russian nuns nearly forty years ago, M. de Custine gave them a character for the most dissolute morals. They were as bad then as some of their French sisters in the seventeenth century who provoked Diderot to write his 'Religieuse;' and they have not improved since. They may have renounced the devil, but the devil does not renounce them.

There are only about 7,000 of them in the whole empire, as against 9,000 monks; and the orders of both sexes are scattered among 800 convents. This would give each establishment an average of no more then twenty inmates; but a number of postulants and novices must be added who act as servants to those who have taken their vows. The four great lauras, as the large monasteries are called, contain about 150 monks apiece; two of the first-class nunneries have more than one hundred sisters; but many country-town conventual institutions boast but

three or four friars or nuns, who are all scandalously
fat and rich, and lead lives which one might think
would tempt the lazy and good-for-nought among the
people to look upon them with envy.

It is just the contrary, and the monastic orders are
extremely difficult to recruit, notwithstanding that the
bishops resort to coaxing and even to coercion for the
purpose. Originally a man could only become a monk
at thirty and a woman a nun at forty; and postulants
for orders were obliged to prove that they were of
noble or ecclesiastical family; but these conditions
have been abrogated, and nothing is required now
but a knowledge of reading and writing. Vows are
not eternal either, but may be recanted after formalities which can be much simplified by the customary national talisman of a bribe in the proper
quarters. On the other hand, monks and nuns are
constrained to celibacy; they lose what property they
possessed as civilians (it goes to their heirs, as if they
were dead), and if they re-enter civil life they are
debarred during a term of seven years from entering
the service of the Crown, inheriting or buying land,
or inhabiting the cities of St. Petersburg and Moscow.

It may be that these rules have something to do
with the repugnance of Russians for monastic life,
but one must rather attribute the feeling to the

universal abhorrence and contempt in which the 'black clergy' are held. They are wealthy, powerful, and arrogant, but pariahs for all that. However, a Russian who can surmount his objection to enter an execrated caste finds his lines cast in very pleasant places. All the high dignitaries of the Church—metropolitans, archbishops, archimandrites, abbots, and priors—are chosen from among the monks ; and the nuns can rise to such dignities as abbesses, prioresses, and holy mothers. It is computed that the abbots of the lauras pocket £10,000 a year apiece, and those of the smaller monasteries at least £2,000. The abbesses are equally well off. About a year ago one who had held her office ten years created a scandal by going off to France without leave to get married, and the *Moscow Gazette* revealed that she had amassed more than a million of roubles.

All this money is earned through the gross super-stition which in Russia does duty for religion. Monks and nuns sell tapers, holy relics, images, wedding-rings, and indulgences ; they sell prayers, blessings, and the right of burial within monasteries, which wealthy Russians prize highly and for which they pay by sums bequeathed in their wills. It is seldom that a Russian of high rank is buried elsewhere than in a convent. Then the monks are sturdy beggars, and it is considered unlucky to send them away empty-handed. They knock at every door; and turn to account every domestic event which may induce generosity—weddings, christenings, windfalls of money, or promotion in the service. They have been known to call upon fashionable gamblers who were reported to have won largely at cards, and upon opera-songstresses who had been lucky in the matter of diamonds. A rich foreigner, alighting at a fashionable hotel, is waited upon by a monk who begs for a charity; if he give readily a nun comes on the morrow, then another monk, a second nun and so on—all bearing the same stereotyped smile of abject humility. Towards the rich they are obsequious, with persons of the middle-class familiar, to the poor insolent; but, whatever contempt may be felt for them by boyard or mujick, no one cares to cross them, for it is as true in Russia to-day as it was in England before the Reformation that 'if you do but speak ill of a friar's dog, a thousand monks exclaim " An heresy! an heresy!"'

If monastic property had remained inviolate through centuries, the Russian orders would by this time own half the land in the country; but Peter the Great, Elizabeth, and Catherine II. all laid ruthless hands upon their estates, and for this reason monks no longer care to be presented with lands. Offer some productive acres to an abbot, and he will tell you plainly that he prefers cash or jewels, as 'easier to distribute among the poor,' the truth being that the friars never give away a kopeck. They live subject to no rule, and do not even eat or pray in common.

Enter the laura of Troitza, some sixty miles from Moscow, which is the largest monastery of the country, and you find a regular city full of churches and image-shops. There are no fewer than five-and-forty churches within the walls, some large, some small, but all full of the tombs of noblemen, and also of shrines amazingly rich and beautiful. The chapel of St. Serge, the founder of the order, is one mass of gold, diamonds, and emeralds, which will sorely tempt the cupidity of the Government whenever Russia gets a needy ruler bold enough to brave the prejudice which has hitherto held monastic jewels more sacred than monastic lands.

The monks of the Troitza live in the image-shops, each according to his fancy; and it is generally understood that after remitting half the earnings of their beggary and pious sales to the abbot, they may keep the rest for themselves. They all wear long black gowns, with rope girdles and flowing beards, and they are waited upon, as above said, by the postulants, who are trained to religious habits by carousing in their company. Not so long ago it was the custom to recruit the ranks of monkery by regularly impressing some of the worst-behaved pupils in the four ecclesiastical academies of St. Petersburg, Moscow, Kiew, and Kazan; but nowadays bishops institute inquiries as to schoolboys and university students who have a taste for study and disputation, and interest is brought to bear upon their parents, who send the lads to be cowled often sorely against their will.

Some few sons of clergymen take the habit from ambition, and some noblemen's sons for the purpose of enriching their ruined families; and there is a percentage of monks who were popes, but became disqualified from holding benefices owing to the deaths of their wives. No man, however, becomes a friar in Russia from ardent spiritual vocation or from disenchantment at the vanities of this world ; for the monkish life is one of money-making, turbulent imposture, intrigue, and notorious licence. M. Katkoff, who cannot be suspected of iconoclastic proclivities, has over and over again clamoured for the abolition of the monasteries and the appropriation of their property to educational purposes. He forgets, however, that a great deal of this property, being portable, would melt away with startling suddenness if there were any serious rumours of disestablishment.

The Government has no present intention of meddling with the black clergy, because they serve it too well. The monks and nuns act as spies and propagators of religious fanaticism, which is often useful for political purposes. Despised as they are, the superstition which brings so much money into their hands is a great force ; and they can work it like a lever for the doing of mighty things. Nothing is more incomprehensible than the sentiment which makes a Russian grovel before a holy image while he sneers at the church servant who carries it ; but it is a fact that the evil reputation which monks and nuns enjoy, and deserve, does not prevent them from bowing the necks of the haughtiest boyards and worming all their secrets out of them. For instance, if a lady of rank falls ill, a nun presents herself as nurse, and is admitted without parley, because public opinion would accuse the lady's husband of heartless indifference to his wife's recovery if he turned away a woman whose presence would bring divine blessing into the house. Of course the nun does no nursing, but she feeds well, mumbles some prayers by the patient's bedside, and works upon her superstitious terrors with a plausibility bred of long practice. Before she leaves the house she knows all about its concerns ; and that knowledge is soon conveyed, if needful, to the police office.

So it is with the monks, who visit hospitals, fairs, schools, and barracks. Russians are quite aware that the inviolability of confession as understood by their clergy, but especially by the black clergy, is a mockery: but this does not make them more reticent; for they speak out of a terrified feeling that the un-worthiness of the minister has nothing to do with the sacredness of his office, and that to tell a monk un-truths would be to court ill-luck. That dread of ill-luck, which makes a Russian wear turquoises and ban opals, carry a bit of scarlet cloth in his pocket and start if he upsets a spoonful of salt, acts as efficiently upon the free-thinker as upon the Old Muscovite who believes that the dry bones in the catacombs of Kiew come to life every year on the feast of St. Paul at midnight.

A Russian may scoff at the powers above, but he has a great respect for those below ; and the theology which bishops inculcate both in the pulpit and in the boudoirs, where they are admitted because of the tattle they would retail if kept out, is largely descriptive of pranks which Satan plays upon the unfaithful by the agency of ghosts, apparitions, crosses in love, and money. When the Government were minded to embark in the Turkish war, the clergy were ordered to kindle public enthusiasm for a crusade against the infidel Turk; and they did so with remarkable zeal and unanimity. The pious movement, begun in the Empress's drawing-room through the metropolitan of St. Petersburg, was carried into all the drawing-rooms of the nobility by the archimandrites, and among the people by the monks and nuns, who took care to be no losers by the general outburst of orthodox piety. For weeks and months the convent churches were crowded with officers and soldiers, who brought their swords or bayonets to be blessed by being placed, for money, upon some shrine; and so long as the war lasted the wives and mothers of the unlucky men at the seat of war were pouring more and more money into the hands of the monks by the purchase of amulets, to render their beloved ones invulnerable. Religion is a paying concern when conducted in this way.

CHAPTER XVII.

SOCIETY.

RUSSIANS are extremely sensitive to the opinion of foreigners ; and this renders them amiable to a point which quite charms a stranger on his first arrival in the country. The stranger's second impression, formed at the end of a week or two, is that there is a good deal of acting in the society-manners of his hosts ; his third, which begins to shape itself towards the close of a month, is that he has heard an uncommon number of untruths. The humility with which Russians affect to speak of the backwardness of their country covers a deep feeling of pride in its strength ; and while they seem to invite criticism, they really resent it.

This appears when a Russian has become sufficiently intimate with you to throw off the mask and challenge comparisons between your country and his ; then he brags of his superiority with brutal bluntness. His Czar is popular ; his country wonderfully advanced, considering the drawbacks of climate ; his army is the largest and finest going ; and the people are religious and contented, which is more than can be said of those in other States which he has visited. A Russian's dislike for despotism, as expressed in drawing-room conversations, comes chiefly from the fact that despotism is unfashionable abroad ; so that the advocacy of it seems ridiculous to cultivated foreigners. A Russian is also afraid that any apology for autocracy coming from his lips might be construed into a servile fear of his masters ; so that he forces his liberal utterances to a pitch which is often extravagant. In pursuance of the same spirit he dabbles in conspiracies, and would join in a revolution without having any clear end in view, but simply under the belief that he was discharging his duties as an enlightened being according to Western notions.

Fashion is the upper class Russian's god, and all his efforts tend to show strangers that he is on a level with the latest theories in politics, religion, and social ethics. He is the most difficult creature to instruct, because he professes to know everything ; and he is hard to learn from, because he invents with unblushing effrontery. A visitor in Russia must believe a tenth of what he hears, and keep his eyes about him; then he soon comes to the conclusion that if Russians were what they affect to be, their country would not be what it is.

All that has been written for politico-sentimental purposes as to the Russian's love of fair play is pleasant nonsense; for chivalry of conduct is not compatible with the total absence of moral rectitude and entire scepticism as to the value of truth. A Russian will talk like a Bayard, because he has learned to do so in books; and he will out of vanity do splendidly ostentatious things; but he is impact with the treachery of the Greek and Tartar races, and both in love and war will compass by stratagem what he cannot win by might.

As to humanitarianism, the kindness of a people may be pretty accurately gauged by its treatment of political offenders; and it is enough to say on this head that no Russian seems to have any notion that punishment should be proportioned to an offence. Tell a boyard that you have seen prisoners who have lain for a couple of years in a foul gaol awaiting trial and he will answer naïvely that they were 'accused of conspiracy,' as if the mere fact of their being under suspicion was a sufficient excuse for any indignity or hardship that could be inflicted on them. There are plenty of Russians who, in Nicholas's reign, have seen women knouted to death for seditious words ; but the recollection has left no such shocking impression on their minds as it must have done if the sympathy which they claim to feel for the 'oppressed Christians' were anything better than a mockery.

Russian hospitality is dazzling. The entertainments which are given by the richest nobles in St. Petersburg excel anything that can be seen elsewhere, because nowhere else can people afford to spend so much upon show. The rich in Western States have claims upon their fortunes, and spend a good deal in improving their estates ; but a Russian draws all he can from his land and gives back little or nothing. He disburses prodigally for wines, music, diamonds, and rich dresses for his wife ; he keeps an immense retinue of servants ; gambles largely, whatever may be his age or profession ; and the surplus of his income goes to defray journeys to Paris, Nice, and the German watering-places, where he seems to set his ambition on enriching hotel-keepers.

Art is but little patronized, and it may even be doubted whether Russians are so fond of music as they seem to be, for the music one hears at concerts and operas is always the newest, and for old there is no demand. Gounod and Lecocq are mentioned in the same breath, as if they were composers of equal excellence ; and during the ephemeral craze for Wagner, Meyerbeer and Mozart were alluded to as though their reign had definitively vanished.

No man catches the cant of a passing Western fashion so fast as a Russian ; but he can seldom attune himself to foreign thought, so that all his tact in observing strangers does not save him from occasionally committing amusing blunders when he talks of things about which he affects to know much more than he really does. In this respect the faultless accent of Russians in speaking foreign languages (which comes from the multitude of consonances which they have to master in learning their own) is apt to blind one to their ignorance of the spirit of the tongues which they prattle so well. It is their own fault if one remarks this ; for if they were content to be and to seem Russians they might still claim credit for being the best linguists in the world : it is only because they aspire to be thought ' Parisians of the North ' that one is forced to see that they have only the outer varnish of their models. However, Russians of the upper classes are in general very well educated, and if they continued to instruct themselves after leaving their private tutors, they would be the most accomplished aristocracy in Europe. Unfortunately the young boyard, whose attainments at twenty excite surprise and admiration, has learned nothing more at thirty, and at forty has unlearned much, and settled into the grooves of official thought.

This rule is universal ; there are scarcely any exceptions to it. Many a young Russian who has been admirably brought up at home by French and German masters starts in life with ardent hopes and generous desires to aid in righting some of the abuses which he sees ; but he is enrolled in the Tschinn as an officer or Civil servant, and soon learns that originality of thought is dangerous. If he persists in airing crotchets of reform after his relatives have all adjured him to keep quiet, St. Petersburg will become too hot to hold him, and his ultimate fate will be exile to the Caucasus, if not something worse. A man may be a frondeur in Russia so long as he confines himself to talking ; the instant he shows himself bent upon action there is an end of him, socially speaking.

The strength of the German element in Russian government has much to do with the perpetuation of this state of things ; for if the genuine Muscovites had their country to themselves they could hardly command energy enough to rule it with an iron hand and prevent it from going to pieces. The Russian has Oriental qualities as well as vices. He is good-

humoured and indolent ; he will not oppress as a
system, but only if he have an immediate interest in
doing so ; his vanity makes him dignified, and he will
not brook much snubbing ; so that he abandons all
the posts of official drudgery to the more patient,
plodding Germans, who will submit to anything
provided they can only force their way up slowly and
surely.

The number of Germans in the Tschinn is enormous, and, while they leave the brilliant show appointments to the Russians, they fill all the situa-
tions where power is wielded covertly. The Ministers
of State, governors of provinces, and generals of
divisions are Russians ; but the permanent clerks of
departments, the governors' secretaries, and the officers
of the military staffs are mostly Germans; consequently a man cannot assail an abuse without
attacking a German and bringing up a host of the
latter's countrymen to the rescue. The consciousness
of this induces many Russians to speak of their
Government as if it were a thing in which they had
no part or parcel ; and it accounts for the number of
conspiracies fomented by men who profess loyalty to
the Czar, but declare themselves to be aiming at the
overthrow of the official clique by whom their monarch
is held in bondage.

Of course these conspiracies fail miserably, and it is only very guileless enthusiasts who could expect them to succeed, considering the power of the police system which rests in German hands. The cautious old-stock Russians hold aloof from such things, and resign themselves to a trust in Providence for the remedying of such evils as they may individually deplore. Meanwhile the depravity of Russian society proceeds from the enforced idleness of its richest members. Being allowed no initiative in any matter of reform, political or social—afraid to act, afraid to disturb anybody, confined to intrigue or frivolous Court duties—they are consumed with ennui, and seek in extravagance, licentiousness, and sensationalism a relief from the overpowering monotony of existence. Nature has endowed many of them with brilliant gifts, but Government compression dwarfs their moral growth and causes them to remain big children, whose only object is to amuse and be amused, to *pose* and evoke from foreigners if not real admiration at least wonder and benevolent flattery.

CHAPTER XVIII.

THE GOVERNMENT OF POLAND.

SENTIMENTAL admirers of Russian policy would be much assisted in forming a conclusion as to the happiness that awaits any Eastern provinces which the Holy Empire may conquer if they would first visit Russian Poland. A preliminary journey to Posen and Gallicia, belonging respectively to Germany and Austria, would be desirable, because else the sentimentalist might fancy that the things to be witnessed in and around Warsaw are but hardships inseparable from foreign domination. The Prussian and Austrian Poles are, however, as much conquered peoples as their countrymen under Russian sway ; and if it be necessary to persecute the latter then it might be justifiable to grind down the former also, and by a similar process of reasoning Germany could not do otherwise than brutally oppress the lately annexed populations of Alsace-Lorraine. But it may be safely said that if the Alsace-Lorrainers had been made to

endure one thousandth part of what the Russian
Poles have suffered and are suffering now, every
Englishman would exclaim in disgust ; and there is
not a man of heart in this country who would find a
word to excuse the authors of such iniquity.

Russian cruelty has only been seen dimly through
a haze, because Poland is far off and the means of
collecting information there are few and precarious.
There is no independent Polish press. A Pole who
should write letters from Warsaw to Western newspapers would soon be detected and sent to Siberia.
If an Englishman visits Poland as a tourist, he finds
the natives fearful to speak the truth, for they well
know what it might cost them to do so ; whence he
falls back for his facts upon the polite Russian officials,
who are always communicative about things to their
own advantage, and perhaps he goes away with the
impression that, since the Poles continue to buy and
sell and are not flogged in the streets, they cannot be
so wretched after all. Nevertheless, books full of
fearful records have been published by Polish gentlemen of unimpeachable good faith, and the extoller of
Russian chivalry might learn the truth from them if
he pleased. He might also learn it from Polish
refugees, who are not scarce in England or France,
and whose tales of atrocities are by no means things

to smile at. The materials for judging Russian conduct in Poland exist plentifully around us, and they are such as, if honestly investigated, would show up the vapourings about Russian Christian zeal as trumpery which it is not seemly for rational men to credit.

After the crushing of the Polish rebellion of 1863–4—which the Russians had fomented for some years with a view to more thoroughly crushing it—the policy inaugurated by the conquerors was that of totally eradicating the national element in the country. Every landowner who had not taken an active part against the insurgents had his property confiscated and was exiled ; all who had personally joined in the rebellion and could be caught were transported to Siberia, and are there still, if alive. Women and girls shared the fate of the men, so did boys. In some disaffected districts whole villages were transported ; and by a refinement of cruelty the rule which allows ordinary criminal convicts to correspond at intervals with their friends was not applied to these political offenders, so that the poorer among them, who could not bribe itinerant Jew merchants to carry letters for them and bring back replies, have been entirely cut off from the outer world. To this day Polish refugees in England who write to the Russian Government to inquire whether their fathers, mothers, or brothers are still living obtain no answers, nor is it of the slightest use for them to send money in hopes that it will reach Siberia.

Once Poland had been cleared of its rebel population, German and Russian immigrants were put into the vacant peasant holdings, and the larger estates were given to Court favourites, who seldom reside on them but leave the management to their agents. The next thing was to prohibit the teaching of the Polish language in schools, and its use in commercial transactions in public documents, and even in churches. In 1867 the attempt made against the Czar's life in Paris by Berezowski induced the Government to dismiss all French masters from the schools, and now French is not taught. The Pole is bound to learn Russian. He could not get on without it, for every official from the highest to the pettiest insists upon being addressed in that tongue.

The publication of books or newspapers in Polish has been made a penal offence, and the Polish works accumulated in private libraries have long ago been seized. The press censorship may be evaded in Russia, but not in Poland, where information is only allowed to penetrate through the medium of official journals and works which have received the *impri-*

matur of the Public Instruction Department at St. Petersburg. Strangers on arriving in the country are stripped not only of their books and periodicals, but even of such scraps of newspaper as they may have used to wrap up their boots, and these are only restored to them when they recross the frontier. Polish boys are educated out of Russian histories which treat of their country with contempt, and at the university they have to sit still while professors demonstrate to them that their patriot fathers were brigands.

Public spirit has been stamped out by this implacable tyranny; but resignation offers no defence against the ill-treatment of officials, for it is part of the governing system to make the Poles feel the yoke constantly on their necks. A Pole who is molested by a Russian brings his case before Russian judges, and cannot get redress. If a Russian is molested by a Pole, man or woman, the latter is thrown into prison and flogged. Polish women have been forbidden to wear mourning, because they used to attire themselves in black on national anniversaries. They also come to trouble if their costumes show any assortment of scarlet and white, which are the national colours.

All the professions, even the medical, have been

closed to Poles who refuse to take an oath which would make them renegades to their country's cause and to their religion, for the first pledge exacted of a Christian Pole 'who submits,' as the term goes, is that he shall embrace the Russian Orthodox faith. Failing this, he cannot open a shop in his own name, nor buy land, nor become a school teacher. When he has served his term of ten years in the army (and no money can buy him exemption) he may come back and till the soil, or work as a mercantile clerk, or enter into secret partnership with a Jew trader. The Jews are better treated than the Christians, for they took a less overt part in the last rebellion, and are not in general disposed to conspire. Besides, they have contrived to remain wealthy as a body, and are protected by the influence of their still richer co-religionists in Russia.

As many Catholic Poles as could escape from their unhappy country have done so, and some others have turned renegades from weariness ; but a large number remain, adhering to the customs of their nationality, their religion, and even to their hopes of future independence, with a quiet tenacity which no persecutions can shake. The Poles are naturally a quick-witted people, genial and sensitive. The women are proverbially beautiful and sweet-tempered, but they are endowed with a courage which used to make the iron-handed Count Berg say that a Polish woman and a priest together could checkmate any police-office.

Since these words were uttered care has been taken to break the power of the priests ; for almost all the Catholic churches have been closed, and such few as remain have priests who are generally in the pay of the police and use the confessional as a means for extracting information as to alleged conspiracies. None of the conspiracies one hears of from time to time in Poland are genuine, for a Pole would be out of his senses who took to plotting under present circumstances ; but it suits the Government to keep Russian opinion in continual alarm as to Polish designs, besides which the frequent punishment of accused rebels is intended to strike terror among the Poles serving in the army. These men never amalgamate fairly with their conquerors. Notwithstanding the precautions that are taken in consigning them to regiments far from their country and to put as few of them together as possible, the handful of Poles in every garrison will be sure to consort with one another and to keep aloof from their comrades, although they may have no seditious purpose in so doing, but be simply following the law of attraction which makes men of superior mind associate with their fellows.

It is this intellectual supremacy of the Pole over the Russian which gives the conqueror so much difficulty in prosecuting the odious task he has undertaken, and which makes him hate his enslaved foe with incredible bitterness. He finds that the Pole remains a Pole in spite of all. He comes back from the army a Pole. If he have abjured his faith, taken service in Russia, and made profession of abhorring his countrymen, he is a Pole still, and secretly hankers after the country which he has betrayed. He remains a Pole in Siberia. If he goes abroad, he asserts his separate nationality; if he works his way by apostasy to the higher Government circles, he advocates Polish interests almost insensibly.

When the Russian police pay one of their frequent domiciliary visits to the houses of respectable Poles they are surprised to find toddling children beginning to lisp Polish, and they lay hands on Polish books and French reviews which have got into the country Heaven knows how; and if they cross-question children who are of age to answer, they discover them to be fully alive to the fact that the history taught them in the public schools is a mockery. The pretext taken for inventing conspiracies is often some seditious word which a child has innocently uttered, and which is imputed to his parents ; but more frequently the authorities avail themselves of some intercepted letter tending to show that a Pole is in correspondence with one of the National Committees in London, Paris, or New York.

These committees are the bugbears of the Russian Government, although, having spies to watch the refugees, the Russian police need have no great fear of their machinations. But it is the perpetuation of Polish Nationalism which incenses the champions of the 'oppressed Bulgarian,' for so long as there remains a man to speak the Polish language the work which they have in view will not be completed. The Russians have set themselves to reduce Poland to a mere geographical expression, and they will persevere in their task as they have begun it unless some unforeseen events should occur to check them.

M

CHAPTER XIX.

ORDERS OF KNIGHTHOOD.

A STRANGER who attends an official reception in
Russia is surprised at the quantity of stars glittering
on the breasts of persons who seem to be of no great
account ; but this surprise increases at reviews of
troops, where colonels are as profusely constellated as
the field-marshals of other countries, and where subalterns are often adorned with a dozen medals, as
though they had spent their whole lives in warring.

Distinctive symbols have been so multiplied in
Russia that every man in the Crown service gets a
cross or star soon or late ; but these decorations are
not the less valued from being common, for they are
only common within certain spheres, and they enable
a connoisseur in orders to tell by a glance at a man's
coat what his degree of influence is.   It makes all the
difference in the awe which a tschinovnik inspires
whether his waistcoat be crossed by a pink ribbon
passing from left to right, or by a scarlet one slung

from right to left. The knight in dark blue envies the one in red and yellow ; the latter sighs to think that there are men so supremely happy as to walk about in yellow and black ; and this last class raise their trembling eyes towards the serener regions where Olympian beings have the glory of showing themselves with a band of heavenly azure blue on their dress shirts.

The light blue ribbon belongs to the order of St. Andrew, which is the first in the Empire. Founded in 1698 by Peter the Great, it ranks with the highest foreign orders — the Garter of England, the Spanish Golden Fleece, the Black Eagle of Prussia, and the order of St. Stephen of Hungary. It is reserved for members of the Imperial family, foreign sovereigns of the higher kind, and men of universal fame as statesmen or commanders, like Gortschakoff, Bismarck, and Von Moltke. The insignia include a gold collar-chain and an eight-pointed star, with a blue eagle on it, which the Czar usually presents in brilliants.

The second order is that of St. Catherine, for ladies, also founded by Peter the Great, in remembrance of the services which his wife had rendered him in his campaign against the Turks. The Empress acts as Grand Mistress, and the members wear a broad pink ribbon with silver border, to which is suspended an image of St. Catherine, and on the left breast a silver star with a white cross on a red ground. The members are mostly queens and princesses or ladies belonging to the very highest rank at Court.

The Order of St. Alexander Newsky, which has a plain pink ribbon, a red enamelled cross, and a six-pointed star, is the third in importance. It was founded by Peter the Great, and sports the motto, ' Za troudi i otechestvo ' (for fatigues and the father-land). All Knights of St. Andrew belong to it of right, and the other members are mostly personages of the first three ranks in the Tschinn, who are supposed to have 'wearied' themselves in their country's service. Next we have the Order of St. Anne, which has four classes and corresponds somewhat with the Bath in England. The ribbon is scarlet with a yellow border ; and is worn across the breast with a star by the first class ; round the neck with a red enamel cross by the second ; at the button-hole in a small bow by the third ; and at the sword-hilt in a knot by the fourth. This fourth class is confined to military and naval officers, but rewards staff services rather than those rendered in the field.

The chief military order is that of St. George, which was founded by Catherine II., and also comprises four classes of very unequal importance. To be a first-class member of the Order of St. George, a general must have commanded in chief before the enemy, and have won several battles. Even the Czar is not exempted from this condition, and the present Emperor was till lately only a knight of the second class. For a long time Marshal Bariatinski was the only first-class knight, but since the Franco-German war the Emperor of Germany and Prince Frederick Charles have been added. The second and third classes of St. George are conferred without much restriction as to merit, and into the fourth all officers are admitted as a right after twenty years of service and good conduct. The ribbon of this decoration is yellow and black, and the cross is of white enamel with a golden effigy of St. George and the Dragon.

The Order of St. Wladimir, whose ribbon is pink and black, was instituted by Catherine II., to recompense civil and military merit and serve as a stepping-stone to the higher orders. Its insignia may be seen on the tunics of Court colonels who are scarcely twenty-five years old. Then come two Polish orders, which were made Russian in 1832—that of St. Stanislas, which has a dark blue ribbon and a golden star with eight points ; and that of the White Eagle, which has a red and white ribbon and a red cross, on which two silver eagles are mounted.

This last order has four classes, and it was originally reserved for persons who had held some civil or military post in Poland ; but now it is conferred pretty indiscriminately upon the aides-de-camp of provincial governors, upon provincial tschinovniks and members of the clergy. When a young officer of rank has got the St. Wladimir, he looks to obtaining the St. Stanislas three or four years later as a matter of course. If war comes on, he gets the St. George, and perhaps the fourth class of St. Anne at the same time ; so that by the time he is thirty his coat is fairly encumbered.

But in addition to these stars and crosses each order has its medal, which is given to private soldiers and non-commissioned officers, tradesmen holding municipal office, merchants, manufacturers, and other such small folks who are not connected with the Tschinn. Thus, a private soldier may win the medal of St. George, with yellow and black ribbon, that of St. Anne, with red, &c. ; and a mayor, a banker, a country justice of the peace may be regaled with the blue ribbon and medal of St. Wladimir, the red and white of St. Stanislas, &c., though he will never be admitted to the honour of cross or star.

Artists, literary men, civil engineers, and inventors stand in a category apart and may be rewarded either with medals, stars, or crosses, according to their merits, or, rather, according to the value placed upon the same in high quarters. These extra-official nominations are, however, concessions reluctantly made to the spirit of the age, and the Russian Chancellerie has still such old-world notions as to the social position of mere geniuses that queer mistakes are often made concerning them. The singer Tamburini used to strut proudly about the Newski Prospect some years ago with the medal of St. Andrew round his neck, thinking he had been favoured with the first-class order, whereas this distinction placed him on about the same level as a well-conducted Court footman. Alexander Dumas the elder received the medal of St. Anne for a novel of Russian life ; but, hearing the small social value of it, he sent it back with a politely ironical letter, and received a cross of the second class by return of post, with profuse apologies for the error. To this day Parisian journalists, who are indefatigable beggars of decorations, often receive medals in return for the articles which they transmit to St. Petersburg, and they wear them innocently as decorations, causing Russians who see them to laugh in their sleeves.

Besides their own native decorations, Russian tschinovniks sport many foreign ones, for there is a constant interchange of stars and letters patent between the Courts of the three Emperors, as also with the little Courts of Greece and Germany. A Russian collects stars as an Englishman would curiosities; and the mania is not an inexpensive one, for it entails a disbursement of fees which are always large and sometimes exorbitant.

Some Russian generals and senators are knights of more than thirty orders; and nobody will be surprised to hear that it is these who affect most to wear no ribbons at all. The custom of going out to evening parties in plain clothes unadorned—*à l'anglaise*, as it is called in Russia—is one of recent birth, but it is growing apace; and now high-class Russians no longer show their stars at the theatre and at private parties as they did as lately as ten years ago. At official receptions they have no choice, but must wear all the stars and crosses they possess, even though their bosoms should resemble a jeweller's shop-front in consequence. This is a matter of discipline—of respect for the august giver of decorations; and a man who should omit to wear any particular order would soon be asked whether he were ashamed of it.

It cannot be denied, though, that the multiplicity of decorations, still respected as they may be by the lower orders, has induced a contempt for such things among those who are obliged to wear them; insomuch that a Russian whose breast is one blazing mass of gold, silver, and diamonds looks a little shamefaced in the presence of an Englishman of rank equal to his own whose coat is as 'distinguished' for its plainness as that of Mr. Canning which Prince Talleyrand admired at the Court of Charles X. The Russian seems to admit that he cannot possibly have done enough to deserve such liberal constellating, so he laughs off his splendour by saying, 'It is the custom of the country;' or else remarks, as the late Count Nesselrode did, 'On nous décore dans ce pays pour éviter de nous payer.'

CHAPTER XX.

TRAVELLING.

RUSSIA is the most uncomfortable of countries to travel in. Such railways as there are run mostly in straight lines from terminus to terminus, without taking any account of the towns on their road.

If you want to alight at a town half way down the line you find that the station which bears its name is some twenty miles distant from the town itself. You climb into a paracladnoi, the three-horse truck without springs, and ask that your luggage may be put in with you. The station porter, clad in a touloupa reaching to his feet, smiles kindly, but cannot give you your luggage without the permission of some official who is absent. It takes money to find this official. When he has consented to inspect the luggage, he proceeds to examine every article as if it were a new and curious invention. More money is required to stop him; then you scramble into the truck again, and off it goes like wildfire, the Kalmuck driver yelling all the way, and thwacking the shafts with the stump of his whip to make you fancy that he is dragging the vehicle by himself.

The bumping is something to remember; for the roads are left to mend themselves, and in winter some of the ruts are big enough to hold coffins. In some districts a chance of being chevied by a pack of dinnerless wolves adds to the interest of the journey; but if it be night a lantern with a strong reflector hung at the back of the carriage will be enough to keep them from approaching. At length the town of your destination is reached, and, pounding along the unpaved streets with a last flourish of howls, the isvostchik gallops into the courtyard of the place that calls itself an hotel. Out tumbles a flat-nosed ostler, whom the driver begins to thump and swear at, just to show a zeal in your service. Then comes the landlord, generally a German who talks broken French, and whose accommodation for travellers consists in two or three rooms without beds and some hot water.

It is expected that a traveller should bring his own provisions; if he have not done so, he must pay for food at famine prices—and what food! It is no use asking for a chop or a steak, for the last gridiron seen in Russia (except in private houses) was the one

which Ivan the Terrible used for the broiling of refractory courtiers. A chunk of beef stewed in sugar
and vinegar and served with a saucerful of salted cucumbers and pickled cherries will be about the extent
of the bill of fare ; though if there happen to be a
wedding going on in the town, the landlord will run
off to beg some choicer dainties, and return in triumph
with the leg of a goose stuffed with cloves, or a piece
of pork braised with nutmegs and marsh-mallows.

As to beds, they are quite a modern innovation in
Russia, and many well-to-do houses are still unpro-
vided with them.   Peasants sleep on the top of their
ovens, middle-class people and servants curl themselves up in sheepskins and lie down near stoves ;
soldiers rest upon wooden cots without bedding, and
it is only within the last ten years that the students
in State schools have been allowed beds. A traveller
must therefore roll himself up in rugs and furs, and
spend his night on the floor of his inn-room. Russians
see no hardship in this, even if they be rich and accustomed to luxuries. They rather prefer boards to
mattresses, and are first-rate travellers, for they make
shift to sleep anywhere.

A man had better not fall ill while in a Russian
country town, for all the doctors outside the large
cities are believers in phlebotomy and violent purga-

tives. They prescribe tea, but drug it without telling you, and the effects are felt for days afterwards. Their fee is anything you like to give; but whatever you may offer they will be sure to ask more, and must therefore be dealt with as bluntly as tradesmen.

The prices of goods in Russian shops are assessed according to the apparent wealth of the customer. A stranger must first choose the article he wants, then offer what he thinks reasonable, and turn on his heel if the tender be declined. Should the tradesman hurry after him into the street, he may be sure that he has offered too much ; should he be allowed to go, his bid has really been too low ; and of course this is liable to happen with persons accustomed to Western prices, for the cost of everything in Russia is exorbitant. A suit of fairly good clothes costs £14 ; a pair of knee boots, £6 ; an average cigar, a shilling. The only cheap things are tea, vodki, and articles made of leather ; but even these cannot be had at a reasonable price unless bought through a native.

In the large French hotels of St. Petersburg, where Parisian furniture and beds are to be had, the day's board for a bachelor without a servant cannot be put down at less than £2. The price of a single room will range from 15f. to 20f.; a table d'hôte dinner costs 12f. without wine ; a bottle of pale ale, 1 rouble ; one of champagne 5 roubles, and so on. Amusements, such as theatres and concerts, cost about three times as much as in England. On the Patti nights at the Italian Opera of St. Petersburg the stalls are bought up by Jews; and one can scarcely be procured under £5. At the French theatre there is often a similar agio on the seats, and the habitual playgoer has to add a reckoning for donations which he is expected to make in order that testimonials in jewellery may be presented to the leading performers at the end of the season.

The theatres and restaurants of the capital are luxurious, and so are the first-class railway carriages on the line from St. Petersburg to Moscow. If a stranger confined his travels to a journey on this line he would go away with a fine idea of Russian comfort, for all the latest American improvements in the way of sleeping and dining cars, dressing-rooms, and attendance are available. Nor on this one line are there any vexatious formalities about luggage and passports. Everywhere else a passport is in constant request, and the only way to avoid exhibiting it a dozen times a day is to produce a twenty-kopeck piece in its stead. The traveller who forgets the coin is liable to be invited to step into the police-office, where he will have to prove, by showing other papers, that the passport is really his and not one that he has stolen.

There is one good side to travelling in Russia, and it is this:—If a stranger be not faring for commercial purposes, he will be made a welcome guest at the houses of the authorities in any town where he may wish to spend more than a day. The civil governor will despatch a secretary to his hotel, and be glad to have him to dinner for the sole sake of hearing what news he has to bring.

This is pleasant enough, and the hospitality is the more gracious as the passing stranger cannot make any return for it beyond thanks. On the other hand, a stranger who settles for any term exceeding a week in a country town will have to be careful of the company into which he falls ; for Russian friendship soon turns to familiarity, and one of the first manifestations of familiarity is to ask the stranger to take a hand at écarté. Then it becomes a question of refusing and being deemed a boor, or accepting and being promptly cleaned out.

The Russians are fearful gamblers, and a stranger with circular notes in his pockets is a godsend to them. They do not cheat ; but play and play until the result is utter impecuniousness to one of the two parties to the game. The women are as bad as the men, and think nothing of winning a few hundred napoleons from a stranger whom they have not known more than a week. It must be borne in mind that the ladies here alluded to are those of a certain rank, who affect to copy Parisian manners; for those of the middle class do not show themselves to their husbands' guests.

In country houses card-playing is the ordinary evening's amusement, counters being used when money is not forthcoming; but in these places a stranger will often get two or three days' excellent shooting in return for the bank notes he drops on his host's table at night. Russian game consists of wolves, foxes, hares, partridges, and several varieties of wild fowl; and a day with the guns leads to a turn out of all the rabble doggery of the country. All the mujicks round about leave their work to see the sport, and almost everyone brings a dog with him. Happily, the game is not wild, else it would be all scared away by the frantic shouts raised by the peasant every time a bird rises on the line of sight or a grey fox slinks away down a furrow.

Another favourite country-house amusement is dancing, and a foreigner will be delighted by the pretty jigs which Russian ladies dance with scarves or shawls something after the fashion of the *almées.*

They will sing, too, accompanying themselves with triangular guitars rather like banjoes. It should be mentioned that there is no colloquial equivalent in Russian to 'Sir' or 'Madam,' and this puts social relations at once on a very friendly footing. Tschinovniks and their wives are addressed by their inferiors as 'Your High origin' or 'High Nobility,' as the case may be, but amongst equals the usual formula is to address a person by his Christian name coupled to that of his father—as thus, Paul-Petrowitch, *i.e.* Paul son of Peter; and the same in regard to women, 'Maria-Nicolaievna,' Mary, daughter of Nicholas. Needless to remark that the guest-chamber in a Russian country house is as devoid of beds as a country hotel. At most a foreigner will be accommodated with an ottoman spread with catskins; but even if he have to lie on the floor, he will be sure to sleep, for a 'nightcap' will be given him in the shape of a pint bowl, full of a mixture of tea, egg yolks, and arak punch, enough to make him cry when he swallows it, and warranted to procure him a grand series of nightmares till morning.

N

CHAPTER XXI.

THE CZAR.

THE *Swod*, or Russian code, describes the Czar as an 'autocrat whose power is limitless,' and in a catechism drawn up for the use of Polish schools it is stated that every subject owes him 'adoration.' He has no settled Civil List, but draws what he wants from the Imperial Exchequer, every rouble in which is supposed to be his. When he attends cathedral service in state the native press reports that 'his Majesty deigned to kneel down;' if he falls ill and gets physicked he 'deigns to feel better.'

He is not surrounded with that glamour of awe which encompassed his iron-handed father, Nicholas; but the lower orders revere him with heart and mind, and he needs no escort to protect him when he drives about St. Petersburg alone in his three-horse sledge. Wherever he passes heads are bared in the piercing cold, and the mujicks bend double with their hands crossed over their breasts. At parades of his Guards he passes down the lines and cries, 'Good day, my children;' to which the men answer with one shout, 'Good day, father.' If he calls a soldier out of the ranks to reward him, the man plumps down on both knees and addresses him as 'father,' or 'little father,' with a fawning affection which is not assumed for the occasion, but is deeply felt.

The Czar would be waylaid in every street by petitioners if it were not a penal offence to address him without his permission; for all Russians believe in his power to remedy their grievances by a mere word. He can pardon, degrade, or exalt; he can ruin or make rich; and being, as he is, a large-hearted man, he has occasionally used his power to perform startling acts of grace, which popular admiration has embellished into legends. But he has very little real might, for his character is not strong enough to bear down obstacles, and he cannot endure to see sulky faces around him. He is a doting father, a generous friend, and a kind master. If his good impulses are combated by those around him, he resists for a time; but then succumbs, disheartened, for the good he might achieve would not compensate him for the coldness he would have to encounter among those who had opposed it.

Nicholas had no friends; and no voice of wife or

child ever shook his purpose once he had made up his mind that a thing ought to be done. Alexander, who was bred in the atmosphere of this icy despotism, loathed it, and from the first he showed that he wished to be served with love rather than obeyed with fear. All the firmness there was in his nature exhausted itself in the grand act of authority by which he inaugurated his reign—the emancipation of the serfs; but this act—as bold as it was noble—could never have been performed if Alexander's courtiers had known him then as they do now. They were old in servility, he was young and imperious, and they imagined that he was going to be like his father. Many hardened old boyards have deplored since that they did not read their new master's character more shrewdly; but even as it was the opposition which the Czar had to ride down was tremendous, and the doing so all but cost him his throne. If one of his brothers had been willing to lead the malcontents, a palace conspiracy would have deposed him. Happily, his brothers loved him and sympathized with his magnanimous declaration that he would not rule over a nation of slaves.

The old nobility have never forgiven the emancipation. It impoverished many of them; it destroyed the power and prestige of them all; it was an act repugnant to their semi-Asiatic fondness for pomp and command ; and they have revenged themselves by stubbornly combining to thwart all the other reforms which the Czar had in view.

This short-sighted policy has deprived them of the compensating advantages they might have obtained ; for Alexander was willing to establish constitutional government, and to remove the weight of administrative trammels which prevents the country from developing its resources. This, however, would have involved the abolition of the Tschinn—that is, of the last stronghold by means of which the boyards were able to weigh upon the country and to keep all its wealth to themselves : and such a sacrifice could not be wrung from them by the promise that they might exercise legitimate influence over government as hereditary magnates under a limited monarchy.

It would have required another imperial burst of authority to daunt the tschinovniks; the Emperor hesitated, and from the moment he did so the sceptre passed out of his hands. After all he could hardly do otherwise than hesitate, for every man whom he consulted entreated him not to entrust his throne to the hazards of popular rule. From the Prussian and Austrian Courts, from his own family (for the alarms of his brothers had by this time been aroused), and even from foreign ambassadors whom he sounded, he received the advice to let well alone. Why should he destroy the only autocracy in Europe for the sake of experimenting fads which had only produced confusion elsewhere? The democratic craze would smite Russia all too soon, and it was folly for an emperor to advance its coming by a single day. Let him rather show that despotism could do as great things as popular government, and by such means enhance the glory of kingship, at which it was the fashion of the age to carp. If he saw need for reform, let him reform sharply and unflinchingly as his father did ; but, for Heaven's sake, let him keep the credit of everything he did for his own crown.

Such was the advice given to a man who meant as well as ever Sovereign did mean, but who, if he had closed his ears to counsel, would have been obliged to throw himself for support on to a mass of fifty million manumitted slaves, who were steeped in the crassest ignorance and superstition, and who might soon have been deluded into taking him for an enemy.

The risks were too great to run ; but the Czar did not at once renounce his projects of administrative reform, and for a while he sought to recover favour with the offended boyards by summoning them to confer with him in devising improvements in every branch of the State service. From this period dates the institution of juries, the municipal enfranchisement of the Mirs, and some concessions as to religious and commercial liberty ; but none of these innovations achieved what was expected from them, for the boyards gave only such advice as was calculated to further their own independence as landowners, and for the rest they took care that all reforms likely to assist the people overmuch should be strangled in the red tape of the Tschinn.

The Czar saw at length how the wind blew, and abated a zeal which led to nothing. He had fits of impatience, and occasionally broke out into passionate threats, which made his obstructive servants tremble. More than once, on detecting an act of injustice or disobedience, he punished the offender with prompt and blighting disgrace ; and then so sternly insisted upon the execution of his orders that what he desired was done. But these eruptions were as the last efforts of a volcano which was exhausting itself. Everyone at Court knew that the Czar's weak spot lay in his heart, and that the coldness of those whom he loved could bring him to subjection. He was soon cajoled, hoodwinked, and led about by his weak points like a boy. Sundry placemen who had been his companions in boyhood had the reputation of being able to do with him as they pleased. He dreaded to offend them. If one of them wanted some impossible favour or was huffed at the exposure ot some abuse in which he was concerned, he had only to leave St. Petersburg, and the Czar would mope about dismally for days. These tiffs always ended in the favourite getting everything he had schemed for.

Alexander has never quarrelled with a personal friend. Intrigues are hatched at Court, calumnies reach his ears, but nothing ever shakes his faith in a man whom he has once admitted into his intimacy, liked, and trusted. It is only a pity that the men who have most enjoyed his confidence should in general have been conspicuously undeserving of it. He is not a shrewd selecter of friends. Like many men of good heart, his unwillingness to give pain and his sensitiveness at receiving it tend to a softness which craves for constant soothing ; not the flattery of servile compliments, but that of friendly attentions, good-humour, and kindness. The Czar likes to be thought a good fellow, and the men who have succeeded best in managing him are those who had treated him with adroit familiarity, as if they were his equals and liked him for his personal qualities. A few of these very close cronies— Schouvaloff, Trepoff, Adlerberg II., and Bariatinski—are addressed by him as 'Tu,' and he keeps a kind of common purse with them, allowing them to draw *ad libitum* on his private treasury which is inexhaustible.

He is a good linguist ; he read much French literature when he was young, and he still delights in French novels, plays, and music, but his heart is German. He corresponds much with the Court of Berlin, and is always glad to get away to Ems, where he may be seen walking about the grounds of the Kursaal with a big Newfoundland dog on one side of him and some Prussian general on the other. The Czar drinks the waters on account of a disease in his throat, which renders his articulation indistinct and prevents him from talking much. But he likes to be talked to, and is a great lover of hospitalities *en petit comité*, chiefly after the manner of those *soupers de beaux esprits* which Catherine II. used to give at the Hermitage, and where a great deal of champagne is consumed. All this has made his mind indolent, and he is so altered from the Alexander of twenty years ago that the ring of courtiers who compose his inner circle of intimates have never cause to fear his breaking out into wrath if things go wrong.

Mostly he never hears that things go wrong. During his voyages the institutions which he visits arc placed in trim order before his coming ; and no petty functionary cares to incur the animosity of the Tschnin by revealing abuses to him. He signs the documents which arc submitted to him, but seldom reads them. Should he give an order on his own account, the Tschinovniks obey it if convenient ; if not, they palter and delay till he grows tired of alluding to the subject. Corruption is rife around the Czar, but he does not see it ; or, if he does, he either finds himself at a loss on whom to throw the responsibility, or else discovers that the culprit is one whom he could not bear to punish.

Nicholas, who had tried in vain to check administrative corruption, revenged himself by fierce sarcasm which he levelled point-blank at his courtiers like pistol shots, but Alexander II. never says disobliging things to anybody. He is not epigrammatic or jocular : one might think him devoid of the sense of humour but for the vague smile that flits over his mouth now and then when some droll piece of meanness is revealed to him. His habitual mood is melancholy. A very tall, strikingly handsome man, as all the Romanoffs arc, he carries himself with an erect bearing, looking every inch an autocrat ; but there is a sorrowful dreaminess in his eyes, which deepens at times into a vacant and almost haggard gaze. He seems to be imbued to the full with the responsibilities of his station, but to be conscious that a power more than mortal would be needed in order to enable him to do all the good which an Emperor should do. Melancholia has been the malady of his family. Paul, Alexander I., Nicholas, were all afflicted with it ; brooding as if their heads ached under the crushing weight of the crown, living in dread of palace conspiracies, of assassination, of omens which they discerned in the most trivial events. Alexander II. is a believer in omens, and as he advances in age, the more will his religious faith, which is deep, incline to superstition and mystic musings.

Meanwhile, nothing in Russian policy must be taken as the outcome of his own resolutions, for he has long ceased to have any will but that of the men who have perverted his better nature. In foreign affairs, as in palace matters, he acts as he is goaded to do. He may be pushed to do wrong, but he will think he is acting rightly, for he has an infinite belief in the advice of those who have most often misled him.

CHAPTER XXII.

THE CHANCELLOR GORTSCHAKOFF.

PRINCE GORTSCHAKOFF is one of the most agreeable men in Russia. Those who like him least acknowledge that, but few who have been brought much into contact with him have failed to like him as a man; and those who appreciate him best are the men who have served constantly under his orders. He was born in 1798, and has been Prime Minister of Russia since 1856.

He is the richest man in Russia, the subject of highest rank in it, and ruler of the Empire; nor could anything shake him from his post except a great national disaster, leading to a unanimous public outcry against the Government. He is not a blunderer; he has not had to fritter away his prestige in public speeches, as the statesmen of constitutional countries are obliged to do; and he has kept so steadily to the policy of aggrandizing his country, that if he failed he would be pitied for having been ill-served by his instruments rather than condemned for his patriotic ambition.

Prince Gortschakoff would not have prospered as the Minister of a Parliamentary State, for the gifts which make him supreme at the council-table, in drawing-rooms, and in private colloquies with ambassadors would have been thrown away on popular assemblies. He has none of the bluff petulancy of Bismarck, nor of the smirking readiness of retort which enables Count Andrassy to manage the Austro-Hungarian Parliaments. He talks slowly, writes grandiloquently, and gives high-minded reasons for everything he advises or does.

Persons who might have expected him to explain some tortuous piece of policy on cynical grounds are staggered by his semblance of perfect good faith and by the reassuring promises which he makes in a tone of stately gentleness, to which his venerable appearance gives the stamp of wisdom and truth. His strength is patience; his talent lies in seizing opportunities the moment they arrive; and these opportunities come through the simplicity of the foreigners who trust him. If he had been obliged to define his policy in noisy parliaments, to remould it agreeably to the crotchets of agitators, and to listen to the Babel tongues of factious newspapers, he would have achieved nothing; and as to his inflation of language, it could have been pierced through in no time by the thrusts of debate—all the sharper to a man of his character, as he has no sense of humour.

Gortschakoff is a statesman on stilts. He sees over the heads of other men because he has never been forced to climb down and meet them on equal terms ; and he has the assurance which is natural in a man who has never experienced a difficulty in misleading his fellows, and who has seen all the schemes which he based on human credulity succeed. Many a Western statesman whose finesse has been blunted by the wear and tear of parliamentary life might have done greater things than Prince Gortschakoff had he enjoyed that diplomatist's exceptional opportunities. But it has not been Gortschakoff's ambition to do great things. The work which he cut out for himself was to prevent his country from changing, not to shunt it into new grooves of civilization or glory ; and patriotism, as he practises it, has nothing in common with the sentiment which prompts a ruler to promote the welfare and honour of his countrymen at large.

Prince Gortschakoff is an Imperialist-Conservative, who looks at all things from the point of view of the caste to which he belongs, and who has sought to serve no interests but those of that caste. If the motives of his policy were put into words they would be these :—'The lines of a Russian boyard are cast in pleasant places, but how long this may last we don't know. There is a democratic wind abroad which will some day blow upon our Court, our Tschinn, our large estates, and the enjoyable lives we lead inside our palaces ; but this is no reason why we should help to raise that evil wind. On the contrary, the best thing we can do is to ward it off as long as we can, and, when it does come, to contrive so that it does us as little damage as possible.'

Prince Gortschakoff is not an ignorant man who is blind to the drift of popular currents ; it is because he knows these currents so well that he endeavours to lead them and divert them from their proper course. Few men have done more than he to baulk a nation's advance ; but he does not rashly boast that it is his object to resist the tide of progress like those French Legitimists who are for ever building up brick walls in sight of the waters.

He had a great admiration for Lord Palmerston and for M. Thiers ; he likes all the politicians who have succeeded in leading the people without doing much for them. Having to deal with a Czar who was eager for reform, and with a nobility who were sullenly resolved to thwart all their Monarch's tendencies, he had a most difficult part to play; but he played it shrewdly. In the matter of the emancipation he stood by the Czar without helping him, but once that great reform had been accomplished he was the most fluent among the many advisers who deprecated further innovations on the loftiest moral grounds.

The Czar saw in him a servant the mainspring of all whose acts was loyalty, while at the same time the Tschinovniks recognized in him an ally who would not let one of their privileges fall to the ground if he could help it. It is not too much to say that Gortschakoff possibly saved his master's Crown, for if he had let himself be carried along by the Emperor's reforming impulses they might have both been swept away by the Tschinn; whereas if he had stubbornly withstood the Imperial will he would have been dismissed, and his place given to some more pliant Minister, under whose rule a catastrophe of some sort would have been equally probable.

To be sure, that catastrophe might have affected the Tschinn most; for with another Minister the Czar might perhaps have been able to override opposition, and, by breaking the power of the boyards, have rendered Russia a very different country from what it is.

There is no saying, indeed, how the struggle between the Emperor and his nobles would have ended; and it is enough to remark that the Tschinovniks have cherished a debt of gratitude towards Gortschakoff which has impelled them to uphold his policy with all their might. In home affairs that policy has been extremely simple, for it has consisted in granting the people nothing but what was imperatively called for, in then giving them the minimum of what they desired, and in doing so with as much ostentation as was required to make them think they had obtained a great thing.

The Russians who asked for judicial reforms got juries which made their law courts worse than they had ever been, but satisfied the national vanity by making people think they were now on a level with other States. Those who wanted commercial and religious liberty obtained a reform of the guilds and a kind of tolerance in faith which set all the trades wrangling amongst each other and all the religious sects by the ears; finally, the craving for parliaments was diverted into a safe channel by the institution of municipal franchises and nobiliary assemblies, which enabled people of a talkative turn to expend their verbiage upon local affairs, instead of applying it to the disturbance of State business. All this, however, would not have sufficed to keep the big, simmering nation quiet if Gortschakoff's foreign policy had not been conducted with a view to give the Russians continued satisfaction by diplomatic and military victories.

The Crimean campaign had been a fearful national humiliation : it was an obvious act of policy to efface all traces of it, and not an opportunity of so doing was neglected.   First the crushing of the Polish rebellion was flaunted about the country as a triumph, not over the wretched Poles only, but over France and England, who were known to sympathize with the rebels ; and after this came the series of brilliant raids in Turkestan, the taking of Taschkend, the defeat of the Emir of Bokhara, and the campaign of Khiva.   All over Russia the official papers declared, and so did the popes, that these successes were so many blows at Great Britain ; and people were consoled for their squalor, their poverty, and for the oppressions of the Tschinn by seeing soldier relatives come home to them with their breasts covered with stars and medals.

Among the mercantile classes the gratification was equally great, for the opening up of easy communications with India has long been the Russian merchant's dream ; and in society enthusiasm fairly overflowed, for it delighted the Russian to see his

Government outwit the diplomatists of England, hoodwink her press, and sow dissensions among her people. Truly the respect for parliamentary institutions is not likely to be developed in Russia by the reflection of how British statesmen were duped and their policy weakened by the scheming of the venerable Chancellor.

The war against Turkey will have brought Prince Gortschakoff's fame to its climax, although the only Russians who are likely to profit by the 'chivalrous deliverance of the oppressed Christians' will be the Tschinovniks. It was for them that this war has been fought, and for them only. The welfare of the Russian people, which might have been served by military defeats, can only be retarded by victories, which, by making the Government strong, will prolong the misrule for which it has been traditionally distinguished. Russia victorious means the realization of Prince Gortschakofi's ambition 'to die leaving Russia as he found it'—that is, a poor country for any but princes to live in.

CHAPTER XXIII.

THE CONQUESTS IN TURKESTAN.

THE Russian conquests in Turkestan have not only been the means of keeping the Government supplied with the prestige requisite for despotic rulers ; they have enabled it to find occupation for the discontented spirits who might have got into mischief at home.

The garrisons and the civil administration in the subject provinces are mostly recruited with men who have found their country too hot to hold them. The young boyard who has ruined himself at cards ; the tschinovnik-clerk who has made a mess of his accounts, but is too well connected to be sent to gaol ; the man with a troublesome grievance ; the officer of a crusty temper who cannot get on with his comrades ; the fashionable swindler ; the clever adventurer ; and, in fact, the men whose room society generally prefers to their company, are despatched to try their hands at humanizing the Uzbeks, Tadjiks, and Khirgiz-Kas-saks.

If they can get rich by screwing illicit taxes out of these bewildered tribes, so much the better ; if they be killed in border warfare, nobody misses them ; but, anyhow, Government does its best to make their new start in life pleasant by sending them to their posts in showy uniforms covered with stars.

It might sound queer to an Englishman to hear that an officer who had misappropriated regimental funds had been honoured with a Companionship of the Bath and appointed Commissioner in India ; but something of this sort is done when a Russian good-for-nought is sent off to Samarcand with the orders of St. Anne and St. Wladimir on his breast. Glitter is the great point, and must be obtained without question as to the fitness of a functionary to wear decorations ; for the Uzbeks, who are sulky warriors, and the Khirgiz-Kassaks, who are superstitious hordes dwelling in tents and ever ready for some piece of devilry with their lances, and the Tadijks, who, though a mild race, are cunning as foxes, must all be imposed upon by the pomp of their rulers.

The Russians have forced upon these men a system of government which reads well on paper, but which to their primitive minds is full of preposterous anomalies which make them howl impotently. What, for instance, can the wild Uzbek know of a Court of

Appeal ?   In the old days he used to ride up to the
office of the kazi, appointed for life by the Khan,
and he got his justice cheap and ready.   The kazi
was not likly to cheat him, for he had no interest in
doing so, besides his having Mussulman regard for
the sanctity of the judicial function, and being honoured of the people in proportion as he was independent.   But nowadays the kazis are old rogues elected
by a number of other rogues called elders, who are
all in Russian pay and have no object beyond currying
favour with their conquerors.   The Turcoman knows
that these fellows wrong him ; but if he have a suit with
a Russian he almost prefers being condemned straight
off, for otherwise the Court of Appeal, before which
his adversary drags him, burdens him with costs which
oblige him to sell off the jewelled bridle of his horse
and the silver stirrups which are the pride of his
cavalcading race.

Then the passport system, which has been introduced with all its Russian vexatiousness and extortion
of petty fees, sickens the soul of the Turcoman, who
has been accustomed to range free as the wolf.   He
cannot understand why he should be forced to carry
about with him a sheet of paper which is always being
declared irregular, and compels him to put his hands
into the ill-filled purse which hangs at his girdle.

Add to this the mystification of being rated for the repair of strategic roads which are of no use to him, and the disgust at having to pay a tax on every commercial transaction, even the selling of a colt or dog to a friend, and it will be seen that there is some policy in keeping the Turcoman overawed by the splendour of the garments of the men who grind him down. To the simple populations of Khokand, Bokhara, and Khiva gold-laced coats and stars are symbols of a power too mighty to be trifled with; and they are the more inclined to revere such things . as they see Russian private soldiers look up to them with lavish worship.

The story of the Russian advances in Turkestan exhibits a grand mixture of daring and craft ; but so stubborn a display of conquering qualities only proves the importance which was attached to securing the countries beyond which lies the great goal—India.

It was in 1864 that operations regularly commenced, by the double raid of Colonel Verevkin upon Turkestan, and Colonel Tchernaïeff upon Tashkend. Tchernaïeff's force amounted to 2,000 men and twelve field-pieces ; while the capital of Khokand, which is sixteen miles in circuit, and has a population of 100,000 souls, was defended by 30,000 men, well armed and provided with artillery. But bribery had been at work in the city for years before the invading force came in sight ; and, though the Russians had to make a gallant fight of it against the masses who had not been bribed, it was certainly gold and not steel which enabled them to take the town by surprise and win the victory.

Tashkend once captured, the Russians found themselves in collision with the Emir of Bokhara, who claimed a part of the khanate. The bloody battle of Irdjar in 1866 obliged the Emir to waive his pretensions, and gave the two fairest provinces in Khokand to the invaders. But this was not all ; for two years later, the Bokhariots having raised their standard for a holy war, General Kaufmann was sent with an expedition which captured Samarcand and the valley of Zarafshan, one of the most fertile in Central Asia. It was in this campaign that 772 Russians, who had been left in Samarcand to guard 450 wounded, defended themselves for three days with amazing valour against 20,000 natives headed by the Bey of Sherisal. Kaufmann arrived with reinforcements just in time to save them ; but there was something very suspicious in the suddenness with which the Bokhariots decamped at sight of the Russian general, as well as in some later circumstances of the war which seemed to show that the Emir had been 'got at.'

At any rate he was content to accept the Russian yoke in consideration of being allowed to retain a nominal kingship ; and in 1872, during the Khivan campaign, he did his former foes the service of keeping their communications with Russia open.

The Khivan campaign could never have succeeded but for this accommodating Emir, and it was something pitiful to see the unfortunate Bokhariots, who loathe the Russians, deluded by the fables of their corrupt chief into working as allies for the oppressors whom they had then a fine opportunity of crushing.

Two Russian *corps d'armée*, lost in the desert, had been obliged to retrace their steps ; the third, under General Kaufmann, was also on the point of perishing of privations, but the timely succour of the Bokhariots saved them, and settled the fate of the Khan of Khiva, who was forced to surrender a part of his dominions to his brother-potentate of Bokhara, and to accept Russian protectorate for the remainder.

It will be remembered that Count Schouvaloff had given the British Government an assurance that Khiva should not be annexed, and it is in part fulfilment of this promise that the Khan of Khiva has not yet been allowed to commute his sovereignty for a pension, as he desires to do, finding his position among his disgusted subjects somewhat precarious. Perhaps, now that the Turkish war has ended so well, arrangements may be made to humour his wishes. Meanwhile it must be noted that Russian encroachments did not end with the war in Khiva, for in March, 1876, the Khokandians, having grown tired of the civilization presented to them under the guise of courts of appeal, passports, and taxes upon barter, deposed their spiritless Khan, and rose in a formidable insurrection, which, being crushed, left them poorer than before. Russia proceeded to annex the whole principality, thereby gaining a hundred square leagues of soil more fruitful than any in Russia ; but as a drawback it is obliged to maintain a garrison of 50,000 men in this one province, so inimical to civilization.

A glance at the map will show what giant strides the aforesaid conquests have enabled the Holy Empire to make in the direction of India ; but one conquest makes another imperative, and the Russians have seen for some time that they will be obliged to try conclusions with the Khan of Kashgar. This chief, Yakoub Beg by name and a Khokandian by birth, has been up to the present an ally of England, and he is an able man, who has succeeded in keeping up an army of 40,000 men, wonderfully well disciplined, and in establishing gun foundries and manufactures of small arms. If left to himself he would make of Kashgar a powerful State ; but the Russians have incited the Chinese against him, and he and the Celestials are probably busy fighting at this hour. Should Yakoub Beg be victorious, he has energy enough in him to rouse all the Mussulman population in Tashkend, Khokand, and Samarcand to rebellion ; should he be beaten, or should Russia by other influences bring him over to her side, the southernmost province of Turkestan will lie at the mercy of England's worst enemy, and there will remain but a small stretch of undefended territory to cross before reaching the Indian frontier.

We have given here but a bird's-eye view of the Russian conquests in Central Asia. Some of the political and social features of those conquests require fuller notice.

CHAPTER XXIV.

THE TRIBES IN TURKESTAN.

THE chief strength of the Russian Government lies in its having no Parliament to control its expenditure. It can bestow immense sums in secret service, and buy up Asiatic chiefs as fast as it wants them. It can also buy up foreign journalists who will persuade the world that it buys nobody.

Since the demise of the East India Company, Great Britain has laboured under a distinct disadvantage in this respect. Its Government no longer bribes, and must depend for its prestige in the East on military might only. Now the quelling of the Indian Mutiny did beyond doubt cover British arms with a glory which made every Rajah and Khan, from Astrakan to Ceylon, blink with a wholesome respect, and the subsequent Abyssinian campaign did much to confirm the notion that when Eastern potentates come to blows with the British Government they do somehow get terribly the worst of it.

There is not a chief in Turkestan but knows how Delhi fell and how Magdala was stormed ; and when the British name is mentioned in the bazaars of Tashkend and Samarcand the fierce valour of the ' red soldiery ' is recalled too in cautious terms.

But Russia also has its military fame ; and when gold is used to back it, when chiefs are bought and humbler Asiatics dazzled, oppressed, and hoaxed with fables as to British decadence, it becomes a question with them whether after all Russia is not the stronger of the two Powers. If she be not, why does England allow her to extend her domination over tribes who were not unfriendly to British rule ? Why is she suffered to bully Persia and spoil Turkey ? Why does every Russian brag of the coming time when the standard of his Czar shall float over Calcutta ?

These are questions which cannot be satisfactorily answered for the understanding of a Bokhariot or Khivan. The sly elders and warriors of Turkestan know what Russia is doing, within India as well as without, by fomenting disaffection among native princes ; and it seems to them that the proper time for withstanding so dangerous an enemy is the time when she is still struggling towards the boundary line—not when she shall be actually on the frontier with huge hosts, communications assured, and allies inside the country, whose mutiny must cause the final struggle for supremacy to assume gigantic proportions. Add to all this that the Russians, while behaving cruelly and insolently towards the masses in their subject provinces, know how to make themselves popular with men of influence by a display of qualities and vices more congenial to the Asiatic mind than the formalism of the English.

British policy in the East tends to protect the people against the malpractices of their native rulers; the policy of Russia is just the reverse, for it gives *carte blanche* to the chiefs so long as they remain loyal to their conquerors. The British official in India is generally speaking a gentleman—upright, just, and decorous, but not genial. Having to be on his guard against trickery, he is often cold and blunt; and, being pretty strict in his morals and addicted to religious observances, he is apt to seem a great deal too virtuous to the rajahs, whom he neither corrupts nor will suffer to corrupt him.

The Russian, who is half a barbarian at home, gives free rein to his licentiousness in Asia, and is swift to adopt all Mussulman customs, even to the harem. The Governors of Samarcand and Taschkend surround themselves with a pomp which is not only confined to State ceremonials, but royalizes their

luxurious mode of living in private ; and as their inferiors imitate them, the least official sets up as a
petty satrap, with droves of natives to fetch and
carry for him, and troops of dancing girls to amuse
him while he lounges on an ottoman and drinks.   It
may not please the Turkestaner to watch these goings
on.   It may exasperate him to see the swaggering
foreigners make free with the daughters of his tribes,
and throw his chiefs into merry madness with the
' heavenly sherbet ' (as champagne is called out there);
but if these and the worse hardships of extortion and
injustice drive him to rebellion, he is always betrayed
by his leaders ; and after a brief fight, followed by a
drastic massacre, he finds the wooden yoke on his
neck turned to iron, and the whips that flayed him
changed to scorpions.

The tribes of Turkestan might long ago have got
rid of the Russians if they had been united, and if
their chiefs had played them fair.   It has lately been
reported that Khudayar, the ex-Khan of Khokand,
who was deposed in 1876, has fled from Orenburg,
where he was residing as a pensioner of Russia ; and
it is hinted that his machinations may shortly lead to
a new uprising of his countrymen. Perhaps ; but then
Khudayar is the same against whom the Khokandians
revolted last year because of his servility towards the

Russians. He is a wily old fellow who has been intri-
guing, warring, and trimming turn-about for thirty
years ; and if the Khirgiz should again put faith in
him they will certainly rue it.

The story of these insurrections is always the same.
When the ringleaders are ready they stir up the der-
vishes to go and yell in a village against the last act
of savagery or rapine committed by some Russian
underling. Howling mobs are immediately collected.
The small company of soldiers guarding the village are
slaughtered ; bands of fanatics are formed, who bind
themselves by a frightful oath to slay each their ten or
twenty Christians ; and the Khirgiz, galloping on their
fleet horses from village to village, make the sedition
spread like the flames of a prairie fire. Within a
couple of days hundreds of these hamlets, which even
in times of peace look like camps, because of their
tent-shaped huts and the weapons which the villagers
carry, are up in arms, and the Russians have to begin
a hand-to-hand fight for life, blood being poured out
like water, and each side butchering without mercy.

This may go on for weeks, and more Russians are
slain than are ever counted in the official gazettes of
St. Petersburg ; but suddenly all this blaze, which began like the burning of a city, goes out tamely as a
straw fire. Some chiefs have committed treason.

They waited till they had given proof of their power and forced their foes to offer them prodigal bribes, then they sold themselves, and led their followers into some ambush, where the miserable wretches were exterminated like flies. The treacherous chiefs are seen soon afterwards robed in the red velvet dressing-gowns which are bestowed as marks of honour upon loyal native dignitaries; they carouse with their whilom foes, and peace continues until some other chiefs, ambitious of red velvet and champagne, begin the old game over again.

The fault of the peoples of Turkestan is that they are all too credulous as regards the leaders of their own respective tribes, and too suspicious of the others, so that if peradventure one honest man keeps the field after others have consummated their treachery, none but his own tribe will give him credit for sincerity, and the rest slink home, leaving him to capitulate against overpowering odds and to be hanged. Khudayar of Khokand had more than once authority enough to have led the whole of Turkestan to emancipation if he had not had such an itching palm; but Yakoub Beg of Kashgar is now probably the only Khan under whose banner all the tribes would fight with perfect and enduring trust. These tribes are many, but the Tadjiks, the Uzbeks, and the Khirgiz may be taken as the

P

three typical varieties of the country, and they have differences of character which make it difficult to work together unless they be led by a man of exceptional stamp.

The Tadjiks are descendants of the old Aryan race who first peopled Central Asia. They are fine men to look at, tall, well knit, not too dark, with large bright eyes full of shrewdness, and soft civil manners; unfortunately, having long lived in subjection to the Uzbeks, they have lost their martial spirit and acquired the vices of slaves. They thrive capitally as tradesmen, they make good clerks and mechanics; but they are frivolous, braggarts, cowards, and liars, so that in every insurrection they are the first to backslide.

The Uzbeks are of Turkish origin, and form an aristocratic caste, each tribe having its customs and traditions, and paying the same allegiance to its head as Scottish clansmen used to do. These men are warriors; thin of face, gaunt, and simple in their habits; they have adhered to their own tongue, while the Tadjiks talk a bastard Persian, and they are much less easy to corrupt than any of the other races, for they despise effeminate luxuries. If one of them turns traitor it is generally because he has a grudge against some other chief.

The Khirgiz, who occupy a great part of Khokand,

are divided into two races—the Kara-Khirgiz, who
are mountaineers, with a tendency towards bandittism,
and the Khirgiz-Kassaks, who live in the plains, and
would be the most prosperous people in Central Asia
if their innate cleverness were not overlaid with the
crassest superstition. They carry mutton-bones about
with them to ward off the Evil One. If a Khirgiz has
a singing in his ears down he goes on his knees to pray,
thinking that one of his friends is going to die ; if you
whistle in his presence he imagines you have designs
upon his wife, and must be appeased with gifts and
incantations ; if one of his children yawns he is persuaded that a wicked spirit has dived down the child's
throat to cut out a piece of its heart, and he falls to
cuffing the poor brat to make him wary of gaping in
future. The Khirgiz have all the Mongolian facial
type, which comes of their affection for Kalmuck
wives, whom until recently they were in the habit of
carrying off by main force from Chinese territory.

It used to be thought derogatory to a Khirgiz to
marry any woman but one whom he had carried off
in a raid, and a relic of this practice survives in some
very singular marriage customs. When a Khirgiz
wants a wife he buys her of her parents for so many
camels or horses, and on the wedding day the young
lady is turned loose upon a pony and armed with a

heavy kourbatch, or ox-nerve riding-whip, and her bridegroom is supposed to carry her off against her will, and for this purpose posts after her with a troop of friends, all being mounted. The bride defends herself with the kourbatch, and slashes the faces of the friends pretty vigorously, but the bridegroom gets off cheap, and, after a sham struggle, bears back the young lady on his saddle amid the triumphant shouts of his village.

The Khirgiz live in peaked huts, made of felt, like tents, and take great pride in having their horses richly caparisoned, their bridles being often encrusted with jewels. They are also very particular about their own dress, which consists of leather trousers, a black velvet dressing-gown, more or less braided with gold, and a conical felt hat with curly brim. When a Khirgiz can win the red velvet gown given by the Russians he is mighty proud of it, though his loyalty to the bestowers has to be kept alive by continual gifts. As the Russians cannot be for ever giving, they prefer to persecute all but the more influential Khirgiz, and their cupidity finds free scope among those jewelled bridles already mentioned.

It is through the Khirgiz that political rumours are chiefly disseminated in Turkestan, for they have an Athenian fondness for reports of all kinds, and are simple enough to swallow any fable. When one of them gets hold of any piece of news he takes no rest till he has scattered it to the four points of the compass, and will ride about all day to do this, leaving his business to take care of itself. The Khirgiz are great breeders of silkworms, camels, and horses, and manufacture felt, silk, and ornaments of gold as dexterously as the Chinese. Russia has not done anything to promote their industry, but has rather baulked it by her excessive taxes on trade, and the lot of the people under their civilizing conquerors may be said to be infinitely worse than it was in the days when they were free to mind their own business in their own primitive ways.

For a fuller account of the doings of Russia in Asia, and of their menacing purport towards England, one must refer the reader to Arminius Vambéry's excellent and exhaustive work, 'Central Asia, and the Anglo-Indian Frontier Question.' It has been ably translated into English by Mr. F. E. Bunnèt.

CHAPTER XXV.

SIBERIA.—ON THE ROAD.

CAPITAL punishment has been abolished in Russia, that foreigners might no more be able to call the Czar's subjects a barbarous people ; and instead of it the process of doing offenders slowly to death in Siberia has been advantageously substituted.

A Russian may be sent to Siberia by sentence of the courts or by an Imperial decree issued through the Police Ministry; in the latter case he is said to be 'awaiting the Czar's pleasure,' and no publicity is given to his fate. His friends may inquire for him in vain. He has been privately arrested ; he has disappeared ; but whether he be lying in some gaol awaiting trial, or have been spirited away to the quick-silver mines beyond Lake Baikal, there is nothing to show unless some police official, taking pity on the grief of a bereaved wife, tells her to hope in the Czar's clemency, which is just as though he informed her that she was a widow. What shocks one in all this is not the despotism that stamps out an enemy by a ruthless process, but the canting pretence of humanity which confronts one at every step in Russia, and would lead strangers to believe that these iniquities are obsolete.

Russians assure strangers that arbitrary transportations ceased long ago, but they confess the contrary when you have known them long enough to get the truth from them. Then it appears that almost every man of note can quote a case in which some person was transported by decree for mysterious reasons. The excuse offered is always that there are crimes which would cause too much scandal if made public; but Government never recoils from the scandal of bringing Nihilist conspirators to trial, even when ladies of rank and generals are implicated. The truth seems to be that when a Russian commits an offence which the law courts are sure to punish he is arraigned in the regular way; but if he has rendered himself offensive in high quarters without having laid himself open to any specific charge, he is sent to Siberia quietly.

It is said that almost all the persons who are transported to Siberia, with or without trial, admit the justice of their punishment. This is very likely; for their only chance of getting pardoned or of being allowed to communicate with their friends lies in their making a full and penitent acknowledgment of their guilt on paper. One hears nothing of the captives who refuse to do this. They pay the penalty of their high-spiritedness by never being allowed a chance of letting the world know that they have suffered unjustly.

Siberia is a territory covering about six times the area of England and Scotland. It contains a great number of penal colonies scattered at long distances from one another, and differing much in the degrees of discomfort they offer to their inhabitants. The colonists are divided into three categories—those who live at their own expense and are allowed to have their families with them ; those who are supported by Government, but are suffered to eke out their small pittance by acting as servants to the richer colonists or working at trades ; and, thirdly, those who are employed at hard labour on public works or in the mines.

The miners are supposed to be the worst offenders, and their punishment is tantamount to death by slow torture, for it is certain to kill them in ten years and ruins their health long before that time. A convict never knows until he reaches Siberia what sort of life is in store for him ; for in pronouncing sentence of hard labour the judge makes no mention of mines.

If the convict have money or influential friends he had better use the time between his sentence and transportation in buying a warrant which consigns him to the lighter kinds of labour above ground ; otherwise he will inevitably be sent under earth and never again see the sky until he is hauled up to die in an infirmary.

The convicts are forwarded to Siberia in convoys, which start at the commencement of spring, just after the snows have melted and left the ground dry. They perform the whole journey on foot, escorted by mounted Cossacks, who are armed with pistols, lances, and long whips ; and behind them jolt a long string of springless tumbrils to carry those who fall lame or ill on the way. The start is always made in the night, and care is taken that the convoys shall only pass through the towns on their road after dark. Each man is dressed in a grey kaftan, having a brass numbered plate fastened to the breast, knee boots, and a sheepskin bonnet. He carries a rug strapped to his back, a mess-tin and a wooden spoon at his girdle. The women have black cloaks with hoods, and march in gangs by themselves, with an escort of soldiers, like the men, and two or three female warders, who travel in carts.

In leaving large cities, like St. Petersburg, all the

prisoners are chained with their hands behind their backs, but their fetters are removed outside the city, except in the case of men who have been marked as dangerous. These have to wear leg chains of 4 lb. weight all the way, and some of the more desperate ones are yoked by threes to a beam of wood, which rests on their shoulders, and is fastened to their necks by iron collars.

Any foreigner who has been at St. Petersburg during the spring, and has chanced to come home late from one of the Easter balls, may have met one of these dismal processions filing through the broad streets at a quick march. Nobody may approach the men to inspect them. The Cossacks crack their whips loudly to warn loafers off, and scamper up and down the line with lanterns tied to their lance-points, which they lower to the ground at every moment to see if letters have been dropped. Murderers, thieves, Nihilist conspirators, felon clergymen, mutinous soldiers, and patriotic Poles all tramp together as fast as they can go, and perfectly silent. Then come the women, shivering, sobbing, but not daring to cry out, because of those awful whips. There are sure to be some young girls among them—ex-students of Zurich, convicted of Nihilism, or Polish girls accused of hatching plots —and these are mixed up elbow to elbow with hardened adventuresses, sentenced for bank-note forgeries, and with flat-faced Muscovite drabs who have killed a husband or child under the influence of vodki.

At the first church outside the city there is a halt, and the two gangs are driven into the building to attend a parting mass and hear a short sermon. The preacher, speaking from the altar, never fails to extol the Czar's clemency, and to advise submission and penitence. The girls, the Poles, the alleged conspirators here get a foretaste of the language that will be held to them every time they make an appeal for mercy. When the prisoners leave the church their chains are removed, and they receive permission to talk for the rest of the way, except when they pass through towns. They may sing, too, if they like, and sometimes do, trying to drown their misery in plaintive yells about the homes they shall never see again.

Meanwhile a rumour has somehow got abroad that a convict convoy is on the move, and in all the villages the compassionate peasantry bring out steaming tureens of tschi, piles of newly baked bread, and jugs of kwass or vodki. They set these offerings by the roadside as the vanguard of the convoy comes in sight, and then retire, for they must not speak to the prisoners.

The pity felt for Siberian exiles is universal, and is only too natural in a country where it is by no means the worst rogues who habitually come to punishment. A villager will bring out his last crust to feed one of the poor wretches whom he pathetically mentions as having been 'unfortunate,' and even the Cossack guards show a rough sort of sympathy for their charges. They allow them to take freely of whatever is put out for them, and only make use of their whips in cases of insubordination. Unfortunately, the delirium of fever is often taken for insubordination ; so that a delicately nurtured convict, man or woman, whose intellect gives way under the fatigues of the march and the horrors of impending slavery, is liable to be stripped and brutally flogged as an example to the rest.

The rations served out to the prisoners are biscuit and salt beef, and they must drink when they find water, which at some periods of the march, when crossing the immense steppes, is hardly to be got. At night the convoys bivouac in pine forests, on the outskirts of villages, or on the steppes aforesaid. They have nothing to guard them against rains or capricious spring frosts but their rugs and clothes. Numbers die on the road, and are buried in the steppes by fatigue parties who are told

off to dig their graves. The march from St. Petersburg to the Ourals takes six weeks at the least,
and many of the convicts have to trudge on for weeks
more after crossing the mountains before they reach
their ultimate destination. Long before the Siberian
frontier is attained the paucity of human habitations,
the barrenness of the soil, and the increasing bleakness
of the climate have had their effect on the hardiest;
and the poor wretches plod on with a settled look of
terror on their faces and all desire for conversation
gone out of them.

A correspondent writing to the *Pall Mall Gazette*
lately called attention to another method of conveying
prisoners to Siberia—a method chiefly used for prisoners
from Central and Southern Russia. He says :—' I
have seen in the middle of the day 500 men of all
ages, in ranks of four, chained together, marched
through the fair at Nijni Novgorod, and followed by
the women and children on foot, only the sick and
disabled being in the country carts which brought up
the rear. Business on the " Birsja " was hushed as the
procession passed, and only compassionate remarks
were heard as to their sad fate. They were locked
up in the citadel, and on the Saturday morning as
many as could be stowed into a 1,000-ton barge were
put on board. On the deck of the barge there is

erected a cage 6 feet high or thereabouts, exactly like
a hen-coop, only the wires are iron bars; and here
the prisoners are permitted to take air. The warders
and guards live in wooden houses built at either end of
the cage, and keep a sharp look-out on the prisoners.
A steamer takes the barge in tow down the Volga
and up the Kama river to Perm, where the land
journey to their destination commences. For two or
three months at least detachments of prisoners were
sent off once a fortnight; probably it goes on during
the whole time of the navigation. It is a very dis-
tressing sight to see a large body of prisoners. Notwithstanding the uniform grey dress and their closely
cropped heads, the differences in physiognomy came
prominently out, and one can distinguish those who
have mixed in good society and may be there for
some trivial misdemeanour from those who, from their
ferocious, forbidding aspect, have given the rein to
their evil passions and are undergoing their just
punishment.'

All exiles do not travel to Siberia in convoys. If
a prisoner be well off and have not incurred the special animosity of a tschinovnik anxious to avenge
himself by heaping up hardships which may hurry
him out of life, a judicious amount of bribing may
procure him the privilege of travelling at his own

expense. In this event he is allowed to take his wife with him, and as much furniture and luggage as he can afford, also servants, if he can find any devoted enough to follow him. But he must also pay for his escort of guards, never less than five, including an officer, and sometimes twice that number.

Exiles of this sort, who are occasionally to be met with on the steppes, travelling with carts full of their goods, look as if they were tourists going on a pleasure party. The women always try to make the best of it, and it may be remarked that nothing is more admirable in Russian women than their readiness to follow their husbands to Siberia when they can obtain leave. Women who have moved in fashionable life, and who have not seemed to be particularly affectionate wives, often become transformed by the stroke of misfortune, and bravely confront a fate whose miseries cannot be unknown to them. Those who refuse to accompany their husbands are the exception, and their lot is not enviable, for society closes its doors on them. A Siberian exile is accounted civilly dead, his wife may claim a divorce and remarry, but in the few cases when this has been done it has generally been suspected that the wife had the chief hand in her husband's transportation.

CHAPTER XXVI.

SIBERIA : THE FREE COLONIES AND MINES.

THE Siberian convicts of the richer sort, who are allowed to maintain themselves, live in villages whose male population never exceeds 200 souls. The colonies are scattered at least twenty versts apart, and each is guarded by a company of forty soldiers and three officers.

The commander holds lieutenant-colonel's rank and governs the colony, administering martial law with his two subalterns. In the event of a murder, or an attempt at rebellion, he despatches a Cossack to a neighbouring village to fetch a couple of other officers, and so composes a court of five, who have power of life and death. No communication is allowed between the exiles of different colonies, and if two brothers or a father and son are transported together they are always placed apart. The dwellings vary in size and in comfort. Some, built at the expense of aristocrats in trouble, are decent villas well

furnished ; others are mere huts, whose principal furniture is a big stove.

In those terrible regions beyond Tomsk, and still
farther beyond the Jenissa, winter prevails during
nine months of the year, and for twelve weeks of that
time the days are scarcely six hours long. The
colonists organize evening parties and drinking bouts,
in which the officers and the village popes often join.
All these functionaries are men who have got into
some disgrace themselves, and the private soldiers
are the refuse of the army, who have been sent to
Siberia as a punishment. This fact does not give the
colonists a better chance of mutiny or escape, for a
commander who allows an exile to slip from his custody is consigned to penal servitude in the mines.
He also risks being degraded to the ranks if he suffers
a convict to send off a clandestine letter, and for this
reason the strictest watch is kept on the caravans of
Jews who come once or twice a year to bring goods
for sale.

The arrival of these caravans affords a holiday-
time to the wretched colonists. For a day or two the
villages are converted into fairs, and those who have
money lay in a six months' provision of garments,
books, and luxuries of the table. The Jews do not
object to acting as postmen if well paid, and, possibly,

a governor will often connive for a good bribe ; but if an exile is detected in passing out a letter without having previously corrupted the governor, he gets flogged. Women are flogged as well as men ; and if a wife who has come into voluntary exile for her husband's sake commits an offence, she has to choose between being whipped or being sent back to her country and never seeing her husband again.

Corporal punishment is the chief method of discipline in Siberia. In the mines, in the gangs working on the roads, a saucy word is enough to bring blows; but in the well-to-do colonies exiles are doubtless exempt from harsh usage so long as they have money. The governors are not bad fellows, though drunkards to a man, and it is their interest to keep on good terms with their charges. They suffer the latter to roam within a radius of five versts from their villages, and to kill time according to their fancy. Twice a year an inspector-general goes the round of the colonies to collect reports and bring pardons ; and then the governors have the privilege of recommending to the Czar's clemency exiles who have committed acts of courage in saving life or helping to quell mutinies. Unfortunately, such recommendations are seldom listened to, because it is notorious that governors have often invented acts of courage for a pecuniary consideration.

There comes a fearful time in the lives of the exiles who have their families with them. Their sons grow up and must go away to serve in the army; their daughters, at the age of twenty, have to choose between returning to Russia or marrying an exile and remaining settled in Siberia. Once the sons and daughters have gone their parents see no more of them; but, cruel as this separation is, many parents prefer it to allowing their children to linger all their lives in the wastes where they themselves have suffered so much.

Sometimes a young exile falls in love with the daughter of a fellow-colonist, and then there is a dismal romance, for it depends on the governor whether leave shall be granted for a marriage, and this functionary, acting on orders from headquarters, may refuse. It has happened, again, that a female exile has been courted, and has obtained her pardon just after she had sent in her application for permission to marry. Her entreaties to be allowed to stay and share her lover's fate are of no avail, for a pardon is often more of an act of ostentation than of mercy, and the recipient must accept it in order that the inhabitants of the Russian town appointed for his or her residence may have the opportunity of admiring a living example of Imperial clemency.

Pardons are seldom granted to exiles who have been more than ten years in Siberia, for they would have too much to relate on their return. They are generally conceded at the end of two or three years ; and it has now and then happened that an exile has found a pardon awaiting him on his arrival in the colony. This has served to feed the popular notion, often retailed to foreigners, that unless a man has committed some heinous offence he is sure to be pardoned, the truth being that pardons have very little to do with the nature of an offence, but are bestowed out of pure caprice. A rogue having influential friends may get one at once, and another who has committed a peccadillo, atoned for by years of good conduct, may exhaust appeals for mercy in vain.

The discharged exiles leave Siberia in caravans during the summer, and each receives orders to go and reside in some inland town or village, where he remains under police surveillance. His lot here is that of a leper, for the inhabitants are afraid to speak to him lest they should compromise themselves. He is forbidden to exercise any profession ; he cannot trade, for the merchants will not admit him to their guilds ; and were he to write the police would make sure that he was going to publish his Siberian experiences, and would seize his papers. If he have no private means the Government allow him the pay and rations of a common soldier, and he must contrive to live on that, beguiling his time as he can. It depends on his loyalty, and, above all, on his reticence of tongue, whether, after a few years of probation, he shall be permitted to return to his former home ; but he never gets leave to live in St. Petersburg, Moscow, or Odessa unless he joins the Crown service as a police spy.

The exiles who live in the mines are convicts of the worst type and political offenders of the best. The murderer for his villainy, the intelligent and honest Polish rebel for his patriotism, are deemed equally worthy of the punishment of slow death. They never see the light of day, but work and sleep all the year round in the depths of the earth, extracting silver or quicksilver under the eyes of taskmasters who have orders not to spare them. Iron gates guarded by sentries close the lodes, or streets, at the bottom of the shafts, and the miners are railed off from one another in gangs of twenty. They sleep within recesses hewn out of the rock—very kennels—into which they must creep on all-fours.

Prince Joseph Lubomirski, who was authorized to visit one of the mines in the district beyond Lake Baikal at a time when it was not suspected he would ever publish an account of his exploration in French, has given an appalling account of what he saw. Convicts racked with the joint pains which quicksilver produces ; men whose hair and eyebrows had dropped off, and who were gaunt as skeletons, were kept to hard labour under the lash. They have only two holidays a year, Christmas and Easter ; all the other days, Sundays included, they must toil until exhausted nature robs them of the use of their limbs, when they are hauled up to die in the infirmary. Five years in the quicksilver pits are enough to turn a man of thirty into an apparent sexagenarian, but some have been known to struggle on for ten years.

No man who has served in the mines is ever allowed to return home; the most he can obtain in the way of grace is leave to come up and work in the road gangs, and it is the promise of this favour as a reward for industry which operates even more than the lash to maintain discipline.

Women are employed in the mines as sifters, and get no better treatment than the men. Polish ladies by the dozen have been sent down to rot and die, while the St. Petersburg journals were declaring that they were living as free colonists ; and more recently ladies connected with Nihilist conspiracies have been consigned to the mines in pursuance of a sentence of hard labour. It must always be understood that a sentence of Siberian hard labour means death.

The Russian Government well knows that to live for years in the atrocious tortures of the mines is humanly impossible, and, consequently, the use of an euphemism to replace the term capital punishment is merely of a piece with the hypocrisy of all official statements in Russia.

Once a week a pope, himself an exile, goes down into the mines to bear the consolations of religion, under the form of a sermon enjoining patience. By the same occasion he drives a little trade in vodki. The miners, who live habitually on tschi and black bread, are allowed a kopeck for a good day's work; and this sum invariably goes in drink. Perhaps the raw, rancid spirit serves to keep up their strength; anyhow, the intoxication it brings on affords the unfortunates the only dreg of comfort they can expect on this earth.

One shudders to think of the state of the better educated men who refuse the consolation of occasionally drowning their sorrows in liquor. What must be the plight of professors, journalists, landowners, who have been condemned to die by inches for the crime of emitting Liberal opinions, which in England bring a man to great honour and comfort

on every side ?   Perhaps those English Liberals who
feel kindly towards Russian humanitarianism would
pick up a notion or two if they could interview some
of their Muscovite colleagues earning the reward for
their progressive theories underground, with a drunken
priest to whine them homilies.

CHAPTER XXVII.

CHARITIES.

EVERY Russian charity is an incomplete copy of something French or German.

Under Nicholas, if a foreign philanthropist was presented to the Czar their conversation was sure to bear fruit in the shape of an order for building some new hospital or asylum on a gigantic scale. Architects went to work, the Finance Minister groaned at having to pay so much money for a caprice, and the institution when founded generally did but little of the good that was expected of it ; but the Emperor was satisfied, and that was enough.

The Foundling Hospital at Moscow offers a good example of the ostentation of Russian charity and of the abuses which are begotten by ill-management. The place, which covers as much ground as a village, contains 1,700 wet-nurses and 2,000 babies.

Fifty children are admitted daily on mere presentation at the gate, no questions being asked. After

having been washed, dressed, and ticketed, each child
is consigned to a nurse, and remains in the hospital
from three to six months, after which it is boarded
out, its foster-mother receiving 8s. a month for five
years. At the expiration of this time the board is
reduced, and the nurse must contract to keep the child
for one rouble a month till it shall be able to earn
its own living ; or else the little creature is transferred
to an industrial school. The boys are trained as
soldiers or mechanics, the girls as domestic servants ;
and the number of these young people whom the
Foundling annually supports exceeds 30,000.

There is something grandiose in this charity, and
although the mortality in the hospital is very large,
owing to bad ventilation and unskilful medical attendance, all the show part of its arrangement is very
striking.

Unfortunately, this famous foundling refuge has
corrupted all the villages round Moscow. Peasant
girls who have forgotten to get married send their
babies to the institution, then offer themselves in person as wet-nurses. Having tattooed their offspring,
each mother contrives to find her own, and takes
charge of it by private arrangement with the nurse to
whom it has been assigned. As babies are so much
alike the authorities cannot detect these interchanges,

and do not attempt to do so. In due time the mother returns to her village with her own baby, whose board will be paid for by the State at the rate of 8*s.* a month, as above said ; and possibly next year and the year after she will begin the same game over again.

Thus a fine premium is placed on immorality and fraud. The authorities know this ; they joke about the Foundling Hospital among themselves ; but Government persists in keeping up the institution in its unreformed state for the bewildering of foreigners. It is not in every country that one can see 2,000 babies and 1,700 wet-nurses under one roof, and herein again is the superiority of Russia asserted.

The present Czar founded a big refuge at St. Petersburg for workmen who had become disabled by accident. It was the realization of some Frenchman's idea for the creation of 'Invalides Civils,' upon the theory that a mechanic who is crippled at his work deserves as much consideration as a soldier who gets maimed in war. But the refuge was organized on such a luxurious plan, that idle workmen began to injure themselves on purpose to obtain admittance to it. The place was full of malingerers, who by their constant drunkenness frightened away genuine sufferers who wanted rest.

One day all the inmates were turned out together with a few roubles apiece to help them to set up elsewhere ; and then the place became a lunatic asylum ; but in a very quick time most of its old residents were back in its walls, only they pretended to have become mad.

There were sham melancholics, alcoholics, but chiefly epileptics, because a rogue who feigns fits is not suspected owing to the mere fact that he is rational at ordinary times. The doctors tried to counteract the sham epilepsy by vigorous douches and doses of bromide of potassium ; and sometimes they tried what galvanic shocks would do with a hardened offender. But a mujick will stand a good deal of doctoring for the sake of getting free quarters throughout the winter.

To this day the asylum gets crowded with pseudo lunatics whenever there is a slack season in trade ; and the authorities have discovered that it is best to let the abuse flourish, seeing that a patient who is accused of shamming instantly howls and gives trouble to prove that he is really afflicted.

The fault of the system lies in the lavish extravagance which is used to convey an idea of the breadth of Imperial philanthropy. Workmen who have lived in sorts of pigstyes all their lives look upon the giant asylum, with its clean beds, refectories, baths, musical performances, and substantial dietary, as a terrestrial paradise. Outside St. Petersburg and Moscow Russian madhouses are squalid prisons—as bad as Bedlam was a century ago ; but to these only genuine lunatics resort.

There are no private charities in Russia, because no Muscovite is so silly as to subscribe money which will be handled by irresponsible persons. Government takes the initiative in everything, and issues orders for the building of hospitals and asylums without much reference to the needs of the locality where these institutions are set up ; but principally with a view to having a good account of charities to show in its yearly Blue-books.

So many hospitals and asylums must be erected yearly, no matter where or how. A provincial town which has few paupers gets a command from St. Petersburg to build a poor-house, perhaps at a moment when its finances are at a very low ebb. The mayor writes humbly to remonstrate that the ratepayers have been heavily assessed of late for the paving of their streets ; but he is answered by a report from a Government inspector setting forth that his town is notoriously in need of a poor-house, and there is nothing for it but to obey.

No charity would ever be started if Government listened to the wailings of ratepayers. Provincial governors, again, who wish to earn a brilliant reputation, often go in for a course of building regardless of expense. Many Russian towns have hospitals of imposing size, far too large for their requirements. As soon as the governor who ordered them has gone away they are abandoned and go to ruin or get converted into barracks.

Russian hospitals are mostly sordid, and the doctors in them ignorant quacks. It is not uncommon to hear of two patients afflicted with different diseases being put in one bed, and of money voted for drugs being spent in medical feasts. However disgracefully managed a hospital may be, the municipal authorities take good care to report it to the Home Office as a pattern establishment; and they will not spend a kopeck on its improvement, lest after having done so they should be abruptly called upon to build another on some new-fangled plan sent from the capital.

Government meddlesomeness paralyzes local impulses. If a whole city became leprous, the mayor and his council would hesitate to cope with the evil until they had received orders from headquarters as to how they ought to act.

Monks and nuns are required to be charitable;

and to obey this official injunction they generally have very pretty little infirmaries attached to their convents ; but this costs them nothing, for, being allowed to beg from door to door for the support of such places, they collect a great deal more than is wanted. They are also very prone to convert these refuges to purposes of clandestine midwifery. Hence a 'retreat' in a Russian convent has come to bear a sense not usually attached to it in other countries.

CHAPTER XXVIII.

SCHOOLS.

COUNT DIMITRI TOLSTOÏ, who has been twelve years
Minister of Public Instruction in Russia, is a man of
large ideas who would like to see every mujick pro-
ficient in the three R's.   Prince Gortschakoff, who is
of a different opinion, lets him talk but will not allow
him to act ; insomuch that whenever Count Tolstoï
wants a grant, M. de Reutern, the Finance Minister,
tells him with a doleful face that the State coffers are
empty.

There is always money for troops and Imperial
fêtes, never for schools.   Taking account of the increase of population and the greater facilities for
spreading knowledge, Russia has retrograded rather
than advanced in education since the time of Nicholas.

The late Czar had no notion of popularizing knowledge, but he provided a good sort of official education for the higher classes among his subjects, and
insisted that they should avail themselves of it.   As

to the commercial classes, he allowed them to take care of themselves, which they did by establishing private schools with German professors.

Chancellor Gortschakoff saw the dangers of this system, and altered it. He encourages rich noblemen to have their children educated at home and to send them to France or Germany for the finishing touch but he has laid a sweeping interdict on all private schools for the middle class, because these used to afford a better education than was to be obtained in official academies. A highly cultivated aristocracy, an officially taught, or mistaught, middle class, and a totally illiterate populace—this would fulfil the Chancellor's ideal of a governable State. But he does not confess these views aloud, and baulks education by the adroit device of seeming over-ready to aid it.

About a dozen years ago the city of Nijni-Novgorod wished to found a university, and applied for a charter, promising to raise the endowments by local subscriptions. The answer that came from St. Petersburg was most encouraging, and assured the applicants that the Czar had expressed a great interest in their scheme, and was graciously minded to help them with a grant. If they would wait a little till the Imperial Council had discussed the matter, they would learn the amount of the grant and its conditions. They have been waiting ever since.

It is of no use attempting to set up any educational establishment by private initiative. The project is always favourably entertained by the authorities, but is invariably shelved. If the promoters grow importunate, they receive a despatch full of high-flown language, pointing out to them how inexpedient it is to do things by halves. Their original scheme was either too small, and needed enlarging · for the public good, or too extravagant, and required cutting down. In any case the Czar has it under his august consideration, &c.

Count Tolstoï is not responsible for these circumlocutory proceedings, but he has no power against the clerks in his department. He himself feels a scholar's enthusiasm for new plans, and has drawn up an admirably comprehensive project of national education, which has been 'approved in principle' by the Emperor, and is only awaiting the good pleasure of the Tschinn. Meanwhile the plan of approving great schemes in principle has the advantage of leading foreigners to think that the Russian Government is always going to begin a good many noble things next New Year's Day.

The empire is divided for academical purposes into

ten scholastic circuits—St. Petersburg, Moscow, Dorpat, Kiew, Warsaw, Kasan, Kharkov, Wilna, Odessa, and the Caucasus. Each of these is presided over by a curator, who is chosen less for his learning than for his urbanity as a courtier. In theory he is omnipotent; in practice he does nothing without the advice of his Academical Council—a body of six members, two of whom are retired professors, three (generally) military officers, and one a police official. These people settle what books are to be used in the schools, grant professorial diplomas, and act as a court of appeal in questions of academical discipline. All the educational funds pass through their hands; and a good share of them remains there.

If a foreigner desire leave to teach in a Russian school he must apply to this council, who, after tapping a few fees from him, cause him to be examined as to his knowledge of history. Now, Russian history sets forth that Napoleon I. was defeated entirely by the Czar's generals (no mention is made of the winter of 1812 which froze the Grand Army), and that Waterloo was a Russian victory, Wellington being a servant of the European coalition of which Alexander I. was chief. If a foreigner be ignorant of all this, he is requested to learn it before he can get his diploma; as to natives, having been instructed in these legends from their youth, they can gabble them fluently, and do.

There are nine grades in the professorate. The first, which confers the title of College Councillor, ranks with colonel, and belongs to the sixth degree in the Tschinn; the lowest, that of College Registrar, belongs to the fourteenth; below these are school ushers, or apparitors, who do not count as tschinovniks.

Each grade of the professorate has allotted to it a curriculum of studies, and the lecturer must not trench on subjects which appertain to a higher grade. Not very long ago a master at the Lycée Richelieu of Odessa got into disgrace because in his lessons on Roman history he had expatiated upon the political results bequeathed to modern societies by the domination of Rome. He was told that these results were no business of his. How could scholastic order be maintained if a lower-form master imbued the minds of his pupils with views at variance with those which would be taught them by superior masters in the upper forms?

The Russian professor must be humble. If he be set to teach the first book of Euclid, he must be wary of showing that he knows anything about conic sections. Lest he should forget this, he is made to wear a uniform, and has only to glance at the breadth of the silver palm-branch on the sleeve of his black tunic to remember what things he must teach and what avoid. Not till he can sport the gold lace of councillorship may he speak out all he knows, and by that time he will probably have learned that the politics of ancient Rome are hot ground to tread upon.

Every city in the Empire has its lyceum, and every town its grammar-school. In the lyceums French and German are taught ; in the grammar-schools German sometimes, but not always. English can only be learned at St. Petersburg, Moscow, and Odessa, except by private tuition. The charges for maintaining a boy as a boarder vary from £40 to £150, and at the aristocratic military school of St. Petersburg extras generally bring the sum up to £250. These rates are not higher than those at Eton, but the style of living cannot compare with that of English public schools.

Russian boys sleep in dormitories ; and it is only within the last fifteen years that they have been allowed bedding. Formerly they curled themselves up in rugs and lay down on wooden cots. Possibly this practice still prevails in some of the inland schools. Their fare is the eternal cabbage soup, with beef; and tea, with bread but no butter. They wear a uniform —a tunic in summer, and in winter a caftan, like an ulster coat, with the number of their class embroidered on the collar. Their heads are cropped close, and they walk upright as ramrods; for the most thorough part of their education consists in drill. They are usually quiet boys, very soft-spoken, and not much addicted to romping—having no national game be-that of leap-frog, which they play in a large empty room warmed like a hot-house. They spend their pocket-money in cigarettes and in sweetened rum to put into their tea. These delicacies are forbidden, but can always be had of the school porter for a little overcharge.

There is no corporal punishment nominally, since the present Czar abolished the birch by a special ukase; but discipline could scarcely be maintained among Russians without cuffing, so the professor cuffs his scholars and they cuff one another with national heartiness.

When a member of the Tschinn dies without leaving sufficient to educate his children, these are often sent to a public school and afterwards to the university for nothing; but this grace depends much on the deceased father's good conduct. Foundation scholarships are also conferred upon the sons of living tschinovniks as a reward for their father's zeal in the public service.

The recipients of these charities are required to enter the Crown service, and mostly furnish subalterns for the army, or else they go into the Church. The professors push them on more than the other boys ; for their attainments have to be specially reported to the district governors, and are particularly inquired into by the curator's delegates, who visit the schools once a year to hold examinations. If a foundation-boy distinguish himself conspicuously, he sometimes receives a commission in one of the regiments of Guards, and along with it a yearly allowance from the Czar. Most of the adjutants and quarter-masters in the Guards are former charity-boys, and it may be as well to state that they soon enrich themselves in these functions.

There are few village schools in Russia, and such as there are have sprung from the benevolence of good-natured landowners, and are little approved by the authorities. However, if a landowner chooses to start a school the Government does not prevent him, and contents itself with providing a teacher thoroughly orthodox and ignorant.

In the Mirs it is very rare to find a mujick who can read, and even the mayor has to depend on the pope for the keeping of his accounts. A movement was started a year or two ago for instituting a staff of perambulating schoolmasters on the Swedish system, who should go about and disseminate the rudiments of knowledge among villages which were too poor to support permanent schools. Government, as usual, lent a ready ear to the scheme, but, having usurped the management of it, has done nothing hitherto but give promises.

Now and then it will happen that a village pope, taking a fancy to a young mujick, instructs him, and the lad in his turn imparts his knowledge to his fellow-villagers. But if this gets known to the police he may come to trouble for teaching without a diploma. Even the A B C in Russia must be taught in the official way.

CHAPTER XXIX.

MILITARY ACADEMIES AND UNIVERSITIES.

EVERYTHING worth having in Russia is got by favour, and merit, as revealed by literary or scientific acquirements, counts for little. Commissions in the army are nominally bestowed after an examination, preceded by a two years' preparation in a military school; but well-connected youngsters get their first commissions at fifteen, and are staff captains by the time an industrious student has plodded his way to the top of the school and qualified for a sub-lieutenancy.

As efficiency cannot secure promotion, and as, indeed, a man without connections seldom rises above the rank of captain, few students think it worth while to work. They are safe to get their commissions from the mere fact of having been cadets, and the examination set them is a pure farce.

Subaltern commissions are so little prized in Russia that cashiered officers from the German and Austrian armies and adventurers from the Danubian provinces obtain them without difficulty ; they are bestowed as charities upon young men who have never passed through the military academies, and inflicted as punishment upon others who have led scapegrace lives and require taming.

An ordinary Russian subaltern can be detected from a field-officer at a glance. His clothes, manners, language, and physiognomy all mark a man of coarser clay. He can just read and write, and perhaps speak a few words of German ; but mostly he knows only his own tongue, and finds it difficult to understand his colonel, who affects to speak only French, and the regimental major, who is a Teuton and can stammer but a few words of Russian in the vilest accent.

The majors, who form the connecting link between the superior officers and the subalterns, and upon whom the heaviest part of regimental work devolves, almost all come from Germany ; so do the professors in the military schools. These persons are the *fruits secs* or failures of the German academies, just as most of the professors in the civil universities are the ' wooden-spoonsmen ' of Bonn, Göttingen, and Heidelberg—gentlemen who passed their student days in drinking more beer than Pierian waters. Unaccomplished as they are, however, in comparison with the high standard of their own country, they are intellectual giants in Russia, and make their pupils feel it.

Nothing is more ludicrous than to see one of these professors talk clean over the heads of a class of crop-haired boys, who stare at him with open mouths. Their stupidity confounds him, and he flies into a German rage, calling them 'schafskopfen' and 'dummerjungen.' He asks to see their note-books, and, finding only blank pages, wants to know how they can have the presumption to think of leading armies? At examinations he takes his mission *au sérieux*, and proposes coolly to pluck the whole lot of candidates as an example. The school governor, with a quiet Russian shrug, passes them all, and at this the professor's disgust knows no bounds. But time, and the hopelessness of attempting reforms, sober his pedagogic zeal, and he consoles himself with his pipe and glass of kwass for abuses which he can gain nothing by assailing.

One merit these German professors have, for they touch no vodki. Kwass is weaker than their lager beer, and they can tipple quarts of it without being roused from their native stolidity. Then, having much spare time, they can make up for past idleness, and occasionally read so deep that they are enabled to make a good income by coaching private pupils.

In every academy there is naturally a small nucleus
of hard workers.   Some are wealthy young men who
have been well brought up at home, and see the advantages of learning ; others, poor drudges who toil
hopelessly out of love for books.   The former are
sure to find their industry serve them by-and-by ; the
latter go to swell the ranks of half-educated malcontents with which the army abounds.

Rich and poor who study in earnest become Nihilists, for the philosophy which German tutors teach
under the rose conduces to the grossest materialism.
It uproots all the illusions of youth.   It dams up all
those noble impulses which make a young man yearn
towards the traditions of the past or urge him to hope
in the future.   It is a philosophy of sneer, sensualism,
and selfishness, which dwarfs intellectual development
as surely as it blights the moral character.

The young Englishman who has been at a university, and led a studious life there, is sure to look back
afterwards with pleasure to the lessons of some tutor
who in private intercourse sought to draw his mind
towards lofty objects.   The young Russian can look
back only to the pipe-smoking churl, who scoffed him
out of conceit with all the fancies of his boyhood.
He learns that the world is a battle-field, in which a
man must do the best for himself by hook or crook—

that principles are mere conventional rules which a man must outwardly observe to gain the good opinion of his fellows, but which need not bind him in his secret actions ; and that, in sum, politeness and cunning are the two cards which when played together win most games here below.

All this, grafted on to the religiousness which a boy has acquired at home, makes a curious compound ; for the boy can never quite extirpate his belief in genuflexions and the saving power of icons. These linger like the stumps in a piece of woodland which has been roughly cleared for building a log-hut, and they crop up through the floor of the crazy structure with an odd effect. The Russian remains superstitious while professing to be a sceptic. He denies the Deity, but is trammelled by a religion of omens ten times more tormenting than the one which he has discarded ; for it comes athwart everything he does. He is afraid to wear an opal ; he grows pale at the sight of a loaf turned wrong side up ; he wears a relic in a locket next his skin ; and is miserable for days if he has caught sight of a new moon over his left shoulder.

The life of Russian students in the Civil universities is a cross between that of French and German students. At Moscow and Kiew only does the

English plan of boarding within college exist. The college is a kind of barracks in which every student has one room, where he lives as it suits him, taking his meals by himself or in messes which he forms with others. There is no common refectory, except for the theological students, who wear black gowns and follow a semi-monastic rule. The other students wear uniforms with facings according to the career which they are going to enter. The medical students sport grey and green ; the future lawyers black and blue, those who are going into the army black and red ; and these carry swords.

The most aristocratic university is that of St. Petersburg, where all the members of the Imperial family and all courtiers' sons are entered even when they do not mean to graduate. The chairs of modern languages and Latin literature are ably filled at St. Petersburg ; but Moscow enjoys a greater reputation for law and medicine, Kiew for theology and history, and Odessa for Greek and mathematics.

The University of Odessa is also the most liberal, and was for a long while the resort of Poles. There is some law now which limits the number of Poles who can be educated here, and when the list is complete fresh candidates for matriculation are requested to go elsewhere. This rule applies even to the sons of Polish noblemen who are supposed to be well affected to the Russian Government.

The discipline of the universities is very lax as regards morals; for the masters have no authority to ask a student for an account of his time, or to insist that he shall be back within his lodgings by a certain hour of the evening. On the other hand, as students are much addicted to forming secret political clubs, either with a view to conspiracy or for the milder purpose of importing prohibited foreign literature, nothing is more common than to hear that a batch of them has been transferred by Imperial order from one university to another. Thus a St. Petersburg student will be ordered to Kazan or one from Odessa to Wilna.

These transfers are effected at the cost of their relatives if the students be well off, if not at the expense of Government; but in either case the transferred student lives under strict supervision during the rest of his academical career. He must reside within lodgings appointed for him, receive no visits from brother students in the same case as himself, and is not allowed to go home during the vacations.

Sometimes the Government adds to these penalties that of debarring an offender from the profession on which he had set his heart, and sending him with a commission to a regiment quartered in Siberia or the Caucasus. Such examples ought to make students cautious, but they do not ; although it is notorious that since the famous conspiracy of 1824, which was quenched in blood, down to the present time there have been hundreds of university plots not one of which has succeeded.

There is a simple infatuation in Russian character which pushes young men to think that they can always outwit their rulers. It should be added that many of the so-called conspiracies, which bring such dismal consequences upon their authors, are nothing but childish plots to buy French or English reviews. The student deems it incumbent upon his growing manhood to nourish his mind with the literature which his Government forbids ; and he equally risks condign punishment whether he purchases the Russo-Socialist tracts published in Switzerland, or a London newspaper which happens for the nonce to be under an interdict—say the *Pall Mall Gazette.*

CHAPTER XXX.

POLITICAL AGENTS—-LADIES.

EVERYBODY is aware that in all the capitals of the civilized world there flourishes some Russian lady of rank who helps to lead the fashion and is very successful in making friends. She is not the ambassadress, but she is always to be seen at the embassy parties. She is on the right side of forty, and if not always pretty she is invariably fascinating, and speaks to perfection the language of the country where she resides.

Her husband is in Russia. Little is known of him beyond his name and the fact that he is a nobleman having general's rank. But he is a living though unobtrusive reality; and his wife sports on gala occasions a star and a diamond shoulder-knot, proving her to be a member of the Imperial order for ladies, and one of the Empress's *dames d'atours* to boot.

That this lady is fulfilling some mission as a Russian agent none among those who know her much doubt; but the suspicions she excites in no wise hinder her from obtaining social influence; nor does the part which she plays require any unusual craft, but simply the tact and penetration common to all accomplished women.

The Princess, as she is called, has plenty of money, goes everywhere, and soon gets to be liked. Then she takes to dispensing hospitality to a very select circle. Politics are freely talked at these little gatherings where tea is drunk *à la Russe.* There is no mystery as to the hostess's objects. She is the first to declare that it is her chief wish to clear up 'misconception' as to Russia's designs; but she professes to be doing this from pure patriotism, from humanity, from the desire to see two great countries understand each other, and so forth.

Thus stated, her aims seem legitimate; and her admirers would ridicule the notion of her being a paid agent. Perhaps she is not. Her money may come from her own friends, and it is possibly to her husband that she addresses those long letters full of confidential notes as to social and political doings in the land where she sojourns. She has an eye everywhere and faithfully reports all society scandals before they have burst upon the world. She knows who are the people holding occult influence, and will not mind patronising a lady of tarnished reputation if any man of status—be he journalist or statesman—can be 'got at' through her.

Her heart is in her work, just as much as is that of a duly accredited diplomatist. She is a passionate partisan. All her vanity as a woman, her family interests, perhaps her heart's affections, are enlisted in the cause which she represents ; and it would be as absurd to dub her doings with a bad name as it would be to despise the hoary old plenipotentiary who, in discharging his duty, often uses far more duplicity than she without having the excuse of her illusions.

The game of the feminine agent is always the same. If the Government in the land where she resides be well disposed towards Russia, she becomes the intermediary of unofficial civilities between the two Courts. She helps to negotiate a marriage, or prepare an exchange of august visits. She smooths away little grievances that have come from ruffled etiquette ; gets an unpopular ambassador removed, and conveys those secret assurances which form the hidden basis of treaties.

On the Continent she dispenses decorations ; and procures honorary colonelcies in Russian regiments for Imperial or Serene Highnesses in their teens. She is a letter-carrier for monarchs who think it imprudent to correspond with their foreign relatives by post or through the legations ; and now and then she may be found dipping her active fingers in the pre-liminaries of a loan.

But these occupations are comparatively unex-citing, and our Princess is much more in her ele-ment when she has to foil the policy of a hostile Government by raising cabals among the Opposition. The intrigues by which the Princess Lieven sought to throw the Duke of Wellington out of office are well known.

Statesmen in opposition are not always scrupu-lous ; sometimes they can be misled by erroneous information, and sometimes it will happen that an emotional leader of men, full of spleen at having been turned out of place, and full of ardour for a ' new cry,' will let himself be worked into a state of sentimental hysteria, and convulse his country by his antics. The emotional politican, at once vain, ambitious, and rash, offers a fine prey to Russian agents. He is sure to be followed by a number of other emotionalists, just as in revival meetings when some ' saint ' begins to howl all the other saints fall to howling, without well knowing why. The malcontents, the ignorant, the mys-tical shrieking sisterhoods, the sects of semi-religious fanatics who are always ready to give tongue in behalf of any cry with a mystical twang in it—all these swell the ranks of those who join the standard of Holy Russia.

The active Princess triumphs : her statements have been accepted as gospel truth. The emotional politican has been softly bantered by her out of his antiquated fears about Russian aggressiveness ; and he is truly so ashamed of having entertained such fears that he and his men go about laughing in their turn at all who have not been cured of the alarmist folly. So does the Princess laugh, but in her sleeve.

The Russian agent in petticoats has no need to scatter much gold about her. Human credulity, weakness, and vanity give her servants enough for her purposes. In continental cities she always has a troop of journalists at her orders, and she takes care to have them rewarded with bits of ribbon to put in their buttonholes ; but there are some who do not serve her for the mere sake of these insignia. They believe in her, and value her friendship. Some, more tenderly inclined, make love to her.

In Paris and Vienna she gives large parties, to which the adventurers of the quill think it an honour to be admitted ; while others, more indifferent to social baits, are cajoled by the glamour of a possible Russian alliance, or by that attraction towards Mus-

covite things which is felt by men of despotic minds.
Joseph De Maistre has left not a few disciples on the
Continent who rejoice in what they call the 'autocracy of the North.'   Men who loathe mob rule and
despise parliaments, newspapers, and all other things
modern turn their eyes with a refreshing sensation
towards the country where Liberalism is treated like
the cattle-plague.

In France the Legitimists, in Germany and Austria
the old Feudalists, are always friends of the Russian
agent.   She does much by their means ; and, when
she cannot succeed in making them shape national
policy, she extracts information from them which
assists her in thwarting liberal policy.   On the Continent liberal sentiment is always anti-Russian ; and
this is especially the case in France and Germany.
During Louis Philippe's reign, the Princess Lieven,
having left England, became the Egeria of M. Guizot,
and had not a little to do with the events which threw
out M. Thiers in 1840 and kept his Conservative successor in the Premiership for seven years.   Perhaps
it was the remembrance of this circumstance that
induced M. Thiers to act very cautiously towards
Russians after the Franco-German war.   To the day
of his death the Russian Ambassador, Prince Orloff,
and that engaging lady, Princess Lise Troubetzkoï,

were among his most assiduous visitors ; but M. Thiers was a profoundly astute man, who never let himself be caught with chaff.   His Russian friends must have been greatly abashed at learning, after his death, that he took a quite anti-Muscovite view of the Eastern Question, and that, had he returned to the presidency, he would have let Europe know it.

CHAPTER XXXI.

POLITICAL AGENTS—MEN.

WHEN the bully of a private school wants to pick a quarrel with a boy smaller than himself, but is at a loss for a pretext, he will, maybe, incite his younger brother to go and be saucy to that boy. The younger brother having received a well-deserved cuff on the ears and beginning to blubber, the bully interferes by accusing the other boy of bullying, and thrashes him. This is what has been happening in the East, where Russia, after stirring up Bulgarians and Servians to revolt, has trounced Turkey for defending herself.

Supposing that Ireland were overrun with Russian emissaries, promoting a Fenian insurrection, distributing arms, inciting the populace to refuse paying taxes, to insult English officials, and to murder Protestants for the sake of fanning religious passion—how long would English longanimity bear with such a state of things?

Or change the scene to India, as can be done

without any stretch of imagination ; for when the
Turkish question has been disposed of the Indian
question will crop up, and Russia will begin sowing
discontent from Calcutta to Ceylon. Will England
then be accused of atrocities if, confronted by a new
mutiny, she has to quell it as she did that of 1857–8 ?
Who are the 'atrocious' men—those who provoke
strife or those who are dragged into it, and, being in,
have to fight for bare life ?

All Englishmen who have relatives or friends in
India will soon have to bear in mind that the proportion of Europeans to natives in that country is of 1·to
250. The Russians, who will goad the 250 to rise
up against the 1, will therefore, according to doctrines
prevalent in the Bulgarian case, be fulfilling a mission
of humanity. The late Sir Henry Havelock might
not have thought so, but sons sometimes reason upon
principles unknown to their fathers.

Russian emissaries have been infesting the Danubian Principalities for the last sixty years ; and three
times—in 1827, 1853–4, and in 1876–7—their machinations have brought about a bloody issue to that
Eastern Question which but for them would have
been no question at all.

The question is, in fact, simply whether the Russians shall have Constantinople? Coveting the pro-

vinces of Turkey in Europe, but being long baulked of taking them by British vigilance, the Russians adopted the plan of making the Christian districts ungovernable in order that they might have an excuse for saying that the Sultan could not govern them.

No people were ever so wantonly provoked as the Turks, and no Government ever did so much as the Turkish to allay discontent by heaping concession on concession. In Roumania and Servia the hospodars gradually became independent in all but the name. They had their armies, Parliaments, courts of justice, hereditary succession to the throne ; and the slender lien which bound them to Turkey was rather a pro- tection than a bond.

In Bulgaria, Roumelia, Albania, and Montenegro the Christians were free to own land, trade, and have their own schools and churches. Their clergy was much more independent than that in Russia. The popes were appointed by the Patriarch of Constanti- nople, with whose selections the Porte never inter- fered ; and if the clergy were corrupt, ignorant, and dissolute in their morals, that was no fault of the Turks.

The only inferiority of which the Christians had to complain was that they were exempted from mi- litary service ; but they would never have discovered

that this was a grievance if Russian emissaries had
not put it into their heads that human felicity consists in spending ten years of one's life as a private
soldier on a halfpenny a day.

The French peasant proprietor, who curses the
conscription every February, would have thought the
lot of the Bulgarian rustic enviable beside his own.
The Bulgarian paid few taxes and lived a life of rude
plenty, besides getting his liquor and tobacco much
cheaper than they are to be had in France. No
exciseman troubled him for setting up private distil-
leries. If he drove his cows and pigs to market he
was not bothered with octroi dues; and when his
father died he inherited his fields without paying a
piastre of succession duty.

A big grievance has been made out of the fact
that when a Turkish pasha passed on horseback the
Bulgarian had to climb off his donkey and salute
him; but the Russian mujick who meets a deputy-
provincial governor ducks down on both knees in
the mud, and the Bulgarians themselves do homage
to their own noblemen in a similar style of their own
choice.

Again, the Bulgarian who refused to pay his
small taxes was bastinadoed. Well, the Turks have
not yet had time to build model penitentiaries, and,

even if such institutions had existed, the conveying
of gangs of refractory Christians to fill them would
have been a costly and roundabout way of dealing
with an evil which called for prompter remedies.

Thanks to Russian instigation, the Bulgarians
were always resisting the tax-gatherer; but the basti-
nado was not the immediate, or even inevitable, consequence of such resistance. The pasha heard what
the man had to say for himself, and if he was in real
difficulties he would give him time; but if the fellow
lied—as he mostly did—and pleaded penury when
there was every reason to suppose that he had hidden
his money underground, he got a whipping, and it
served him right.

The men who were thinskinned were always ready
with their money, whereas the sturdier churls, to whom
two dozen cuts with a bamboo were no great matter,
lived in permanent debt to the Exchequer. You could
see them rubbing their backs after their castigation
and running off among their women folks to be petted
and complimented on their pluck. They had a way
of putting their tongues in their cheeks and winking
which was refreshing to see.

If anything, the Mussulman officials were rather
too indulgent, in their fear of giving these troublesome Christians offence. Over and over again has a

pasha been called sharply to task at Constantinople for alleged acts of cruelty which he had never committed, or which had been grossly exaggerated and distorted. The Bulgarians knew that they had the Russian ambassador at their back, and they abused this circumstance to raise a hullaballoo upon the slightest pretexts.

They are incorrigible liars, who sorely try the temper of any man who has dealings with them. If a strong man collars one of them in anger, the creature shrivels up in his sheepkin and whines till from very pity the other throws him off. But let six Bulgarians meet a Turk unprotected on a dark night, and it will be a bad look-out for that Turk.

The Christian subjects of Turkey have never raised themselves to dignity or honesty, because their Russian counsellors have fanned their worst passions to convert them into arrant grievance-mongers. Throughout all the Danubian provinces Russian agents were constantly on the tramp, deluding them with fables, flattering them, exciting them, and pretending to pity their hard condition.

Some came as pedlars or horse-vendors ; others were permanently located in the villages as schoolmasters, and many popes, who were in Russian pay, joined in the agitation. Hearing from scores of

mouths that he was an ill-used being, the Bulgarian
naturally learned to think so. Though he had everything he wanted, he set to dreaming of what other
things he should like to have. He was told that
when Turkish rule was broken his fields would be
worth thrice their present value, he would have four
times as many oxen, and fowls more than he could
count.

The Russians said nothing about extra taxes;
but what they said was enough to make the Bulgarian
feel that the pasha was his fierce oppressor, whereas
the indolent Turkish gentleman protected him against
the low-class Turk, who but for this would have eaten
him up.

Long before the Turkish Government had opened
its eyes to the fact that it was no use trying to con-
ciliate men who would not be conciliated, the low-
class Mussulman had discovered this, and he hated
the Bulgarian with all his heart. He despised him,
too, as being a man less truthful, upright, and tem-
perate than himself, and far less courageous. Sometimes his intense dislike, exasperated by some wilful
insult, found vent in blows; and then he was bam-
booed. Many a Turk has been whipped for molesting
a Bulgarian, though admirers of the latter have taken
no account of these stripes.

The truth is the Turkish authorities endeavoured to carry the dish even so long as it was possible. They dispensed justice according to their light; they kept the antagonistic races from flying at each other's throats; and it is not at their door that the blame lies if the smouldering fires which they more than once nearly extinguished always blazed out anew, thanks to the cunning, treacherous hirelings who were constantly squirting fresh oil.

If England should feebly allow the day to come when Hindoos shall treat her officials as the Turks were treated by the Christians of Bulgaria, she will learn what it costs to try and do good to a people who will not be coaxed, and who have been urged to look upon kindness as a sign of fear justifying more and more energy in disaffection.

CHAPTER XXXII.

ENGLISH COLONISTS IN RUSSIA.

RUSSIA has always been overrun with foreigners, and until recently Englishmen were encouraged to settle there ; but the English who were most encouraged throve worst, whereas those who were not made particularly welcome generally got on pretty well.

Adventurers of good address were sure to thrive. If a man had outrun the constable at home or fallen into trouble with the authorities in India, Russia offered a fair field for his energies ; and if he had the good luck to be taken up by some tschinovnik who had been his travelling companion in better days, he could be drafted into the service of the Crown without difficulty.

British consuls have often been abashed at meeting a gorgeous being with a strong Irish brogue who held some such post as deputy-inspector of imports in a sea-coast town. He wore a braided coat and a star, and was known as the Colonel Count O'Toole, or O'Rooney, or McPhunn. A jovial fellow, of course, and a fine thief to boot, who was hand-in-glove with all the smugglers on the seaboard, and paid a rent for his inspectorship to the Russian magnate who had procured it for him, by gifts of contraband cigars and wine.

He had always a good story to tell of the reasons which had induced him to enter the Russian service, which he would declare, with a wink, to be the finest in the world; and if the consul countenanced him, he was ready with offers of small services, and tried to instal himself as an official hanger-on of the consulate. If the consul gave him a wide berth, he would become troublesome, and go about saying that he had quarrelled with his country for political reasons, and felt only scorn for the flag which symbolized oppression of Ireland.

It is from these gentlemen that Russians get their notions about British tyranny in Erin— notions which find such eloquent expression in the articles of the *Golos* favouring Home Rule.

That same *Golos*, by the by, published two years ago as a serial the account of the Irish Rebellion of 1795, modernizing it, however, so as to make it appear as though all its sanguinary incidents dated no further back than the period of the Fenian nonsense in 1867-8. The achievements of Emmett and Lord Edward Fitzgerald were laid to the credit of Barrett, who was hanged at Newgate for the Clerkenwell explosion, of Allen, Larkin, Gould, and other such heroes; and all this was so cleverly done as to indicate that a genuine Irish hand must have revised the proof-sheets—if no more.

The English university passman who has gone out to Russia as a tutor, married there, and obtained a civil service appointment, is another pretty common type; so is his sister, the governess, who likewise marries and becomes a convert to the Greek faith, after a study of its dogmas, which seem to her ' so like our Church of England.'

In many princely houses there is an English governess, and the members of the Imperial family have generally an English lectrice attached to their household. The Empress, who prefers British literature to French, has always had an English lady to read novels to her; and it must be owned that the position of Englishwomen engaged in Russia to read or teach is one of comfort and dignity. They are handsomely paid and courteously treated; but, if any lady reading this should think the Czar's empire just the place for her, she must be warned to stand on her guard against matrimonial deceptions.

Russians are swift to propose marriage, especially when bored inside their country houses ; but a tschinovnik who marries without permission of the marshal of the nobility in his province sees his wife tabooed, and it is the custom of the marshals always to refuse permissions for *mesalliances*. So the young English wife who had hoped to sail into society on the arm of a prince, finds to her disgust that every door is closed against her; and should her husband grow weary of her, he soon offers her a lump sum to consent to a divorce and go home. If she refuses she stands a chance of being divorced without the lump sum.

There are few girls' schools in Russia ; and if a governess, losing her situation and yet wishing to remain in the country, hunts for employment in the big cities, she will only be allowed to receive pupils at her house after passing an examination in attainments and orthodoxy, which requires money. She will equally have to abjure her religion if she seeks to open a shop or a boarding house for officers, as some do.

Talking of orthodoxy reminds us of a couple of very pale and earnest young English curates whom we once discovered officiating in the Russian church of a town on the Black Sea. They had come out there under the common impression that the Russian ritual and their own were akin, and because 'they wished to learn church Greek,' said they ; and they were unable to get home, in the first place because they had no money, and in the next because they had signed a year's engagement with the local pope, negotiated through a Jew bagman. It turned out upon inquiry that this pope had been showing them off for money, and that the archimandrite of the diocese had been trumpeting their alleged conversion as an important event in politics. The two converts were well pleased, to be repatriated at their consul's expense, and their experience of Russian Ritualism seems to have been, on the whole, bewildering.

English engineers, vendors of agricultural machinery, and tea and leather merchants were to be found in fair numbers about Russia some years ago ; none of these could succeed until they had got imbued with the Muscovite way of doing business, by bribes and overreaching. There was no chance for the man who would not let himself be robbed of twopence in order to obtain five pounds.

An unlucky merchant one day came to a British consul and complained bitterly that he had received a consignment of pickles from England and that the custom house officials wanted to open all his jars and bottles and turn out their contents to see if they contained any prohibited literature.

The consul hinted at the manners of the country in respect of douceurs ; but the merchant answered that he had never submitted to extortion and never would ; so all his pickles were turned out, the officials politely telling him that since M. Herzen's subversive *Kolokol* had penetrated into Russia inside sardine-boxes, they were obliged to be particular. In an amusing novel by Mr. Sutherland-Edwards, 'The Governor's Daughter,' in which the darkest features of Russian domination in Poland are faithfully and yet humorously portrayed, may be found a droll account of this device for introducing seditious literature into Russia inside sardine boxes.

As to engineers, many who have gone out to Russia on the faith of brilliant contracts have had to serve a rough apprenticeship till they discovered that contracts are of no avail without fees. As these fees would take 50 per cent. off a salary, the question soon presents itself to the engineer in this shape : ' Go home ; or stop, pay and recoup myself as I can ? ' Most stop and recoup themselves by doing scamped work, which explains why Russia has scarcely a single bridge, canal, or line of rail but swallowed up twice its original cost in repairs within ten years of its inauguration.

Not very long ago an English merchant, who had lately arrived in Odessa, walked into the post-office to ask for his letters, and found a postman in the act of emptying a bag on to the table in the public room. A well-dressed man, who was standing by, began instantly selecting some of the bulkiest parcels, and fingering them, evidently with a view to feeling whether there was any money inside. The merchant happened to see a parcel addressed to himself thus dealt with, and recovered it, not without protesting. The well-dressed man, who was a thief, apologized; but the merchant learned the same day that if he wished to insure his letters for the future he must pay a post-office clerk on purpose to look after them, and have them delivered at his office. These early lessons in Russian customs soon bear their fruits in the mind of a foreigner who wants to get on.

Russia is no place for Englishmen at this moment, for they would be exposed to continual insults. The Muscovite, who can be so mellifluous when he pleases, reveals his Tartar attributes very quickly when he thinks to curry favour with his Government by treating a foreigner with contumely.

At this time it is known all over Russia that the

English are in bad odour, and that nothing would be risked by snubbing them. So the English mercantile community are not precisely enjoying a good time of it, and those who can get on with merely an extra amount of bribing, and without having to show their fists now and then, may esteem themselves lucky.

Fists are always a remedy against the insolence of Russians of the lower class, and even against petty officials, who think that a man who has the pluck to beat them must of needs be a somebody. But against the slights of higher people there is nothing but to grin and bear it, unless a man would resort to duels, in which he would soon be worsted, for the Russians cultivate duelling arts better than the English. A gentlemanly Muscovite, who knows little else, can generally slash a face with a sabre *à l'allemande*, or pink with a foil in the last approved style, that he has learned from a pupil of Pons or Gâtechair.

CHAPTER XXXIII.

FRENCHMEN IN RUSSIA.

IT was a Russian who said that France is the only country that would be seriously missed off the globe if an earthquake were to swallow it up. Paris is the Russian's paradise, and French people are his ministering angels. He employs them as cooks, hairdressers, dancing-masters, professors in fencing and riding—to say nothing of actors and actresses.

Since the Franco-German war the boyards who belong to the Czarewitch's party, which is anti-German, affect more than ever to surround themselves with French servants, to read French books, and to extol French generals at the expense of German.

A favourite piece of impertinence practised by divers distinguished ladies consists in feigning a total ignorance of the German language in the presence of persons whom this ignorance must especially irritate —Teuton tschinovniks, Prussian attachés, and serene highnesses on their travels.

At the theatre, again, Parisian troupes are patronized with a liberality never shown to the strolling companies engaged at Berlin, and any allusion made on the stage as to the glories of France is sure to be hailed with prolonged applause. Last year the German ambassador was so ill-advised as to protest against a patriotic 'gag' introduced by a songstress in one of Lecocq's operettas. The manager forbade the gag, but at the next performance three of the actresses appeared in costumes which seen side by side formed the tricolour—one being red, the other white, and the third blue. As soon as the audience detected this device there arose a prolonged acclamation, in which the applause of the Czarewitch was especially noticed; and thus proof was given that the alliance of the two Emperors is not one which the popular opinion of St. Petersburg ratifies.

However, for all the kindness which French people receive in Russia they do not like the Russians. The actress who returns to Paris loaded with diamonds and furs presented to her by prodigal admirers laughs at the veneer of good manners which covers the deep grain of Muscovite coarseness; and artists who are employed to decorate the palaces of the nobility soon get tired of the eternal *pose* which does duty among the boyards for grandeur.

There is all the difference between a French grand seigneur and a Russian prince that there is between a good picture and cheap copy of the same in loud colours ; and although a French Legitimist nobleman often pretends to admire the Russian system of government, he never cares to live long in Russia, for he is shocked at every moment by that absence of *mesure* in manners which in France is accounted the criterion of good breeding. Russians who frequent the gambling-tables of Monaco or the Cercle de la Méditerranée at Nice flatter themselves that they produce a fine impression by ostentatiously squandering immense sums, but even French newspaper reporters have ceased to be electrified by such performances. An Englishman or an American will lose twice as much money without a tenth of the fuss.

The French Liberal who admires Russia has yet to be found. The bitterest satirists of Russia, from M. de Custine downwards, have been Frenchmen ; and there is not a Frenchman of any brains, among the many who are employed in the country, but expresses his opinion of the Empire and its people after a few months' sojourn there in terms of contempt.

How can it be otherwise, considering how straight

is a Frenchman's logic, how deep his hatred of injustice, brutality, and hypocrisy? Perhaps a brilliant pupil of the Parisian Ecole Normale has gone out to Russia as tutor to the sons of a wealthy boyard holding high rank in the Tschinn. He proceeds to a fine palace on an estate within a day's journey of the capital, and the first month of his stay there is fraught with all sorts of pleasant hospitalities. His hosts regale him with a bear-hunt and make him a present of bruin's skin. He has a luxurious apartment. Two or three servants are told off to attend him. He is informed that the horses, sledges, guns, and dogs of the establishment are all at his disposal, and his employers treat him on a footing of perfect equality.

But what pleases the tutor more than this is the philanthropic and progressive spirit of the Russian prince, who discusses questions of social and political economy with the grace of a courtier and the spirit of a sage. He knows what his country wants, and is full of noble schemes for improving the condition of his tenantry. He means to build some model cottages and a village school. He will not be content until he has uprooted superstition from his estates, and converted all his dependants into thinking creatures; he relies upon his young friend to help him in this good work, and so forth, until the inexperienced

Normalian reflects that he has truly fallen upon a jewel of a prince.

But months pass and nothing comes of the grandee's noble schemes. The tenantry are steeped in dirt, ignorance, and drink; the servants of the household cringe like slaves, and when the winter season arrives, and the prince betakes himself to St. Petersburg, leaving the tutor and his young charges in the country house, the disgusted Frenchman finds that he can scarcely get his orders obeyed for the constant tipsiness of the domestics. Reflecting that Rome was not built in a day, he concludes that it may require time to erect model cottages and a school; but he ends by discovering that the time of the boyard is taken up with ecarté and backstairs intrigues having for their object the obtaining of some ornamental Court appointments; while Madame la Princesse, whose health is delicate, is touring it in France with a retinue of servants and a Wallachian count, half courier, half cavalier-servente.

Sometimes the prince swoops down on his estate to kiss his children and levy supplies from his agent, and each of these visits is followed by prolonged lamentations on the part of the tenantry, who have been shorn to the quick. The tutor, meanwhile, finds that his employer has not only grown cool on the subject of social improvement, but shows a disposition to yawn when the topic is mentioned. The exactions of some French actress are what now chiefly concern his princely mind; and, taking the tutor as a confidant of his amourette, he asks him kindly to compose a few gallant sonnets, which shall be forwarded to the charmer inside bouquets.

Thus years roll on until one day it inevitably happens that prince and princess, having run through more money than they can afford, announce their intention of coming to reside for a year or two on their estate in order to recruit both their health and their finances. They arrive soon afterwards, they and their servants, in a caravan of muddy landaus poorly harnessed. The prince has grown bald, and his hands shake as in palsy, from too much champagne. The princess has grown fat and querulous; there are crows' feet round her eyes, and the flush of stimulants on her puffy cheeks is but half concealed by a thick layer of violet powder.

Then the French tutor has a fine time of it, for the prince tries to convert him into a boon companion, while the princess expects him to read French novels to her. If the tutor, taking his educational labours *au sérieux*, declines these frivolous occupations, his employers soon vote him a bore, and get rid of him by showing a supercilious impertinence which his French temper will not brook. If, on the contrary, being a man of convivial mood, he accepts his new lot, he will possibly be drawn into playing ecarté with the prince of an evening, after a champagne dinner, and will lose two or three years' salary in a few evenings.

A Russian has no tact, and thinks nothing of winning money from a person in his own employment. A French artist who had gone out to paint the palace of a boyard was once cleaned out of the price of his labours by his affable host, who chanced to have been unlucky with cards at the Cercle des Anglais. However, if a tutor be so unfortunate as to gamble away his earnings, he will at least not lose board and lodging, for his employer will keep him to his life's end if only he be amusing. Of course, he will have to drop all reference to model cottages; for when once a boyard has aired his philanthropic fads for the entertainment of a newcome foreigner, there is an end of the matter; and he is as incapable of a second performance as fireworks once exploded.

Among the minor hardships which Frenchmen have to endure in Russia is that of stomaching the national cookery. At dinner parties you are ushered into a room where a table stands spread with caviare, ham, salt fish, cheese and liqueurs. Many take this for the dinner itself, and wonder why chairs are not provided. M. de Molinari, editor of the *Journal des Débats*, relates that on his first journey to Russia he fell into a mistake of this sort and astonished his hosts by eating a slice of smoked salmon, twelve sardines, and a hunk of gruyère. When he had done, and was reflecting what a queer dinner he had made, he discovered that this was only a preface, for the door was flung open and he beheld another chamber with a splendid table laid out *à la française.*

In ordinary Russian houses you must not expect French dishes. As a treat you will be served with *batwinia*, a cold fish soup, made with small beer, cider, and salt cucumbers. The next dish will be some frozen turbot from Lake Peipus or the Volga, stewed in a *saumure* of rancid herrings with vinegar. Mutton is not eaten in the North, for it tastes of tallow, but hashed veal mixed with cloves and cinnamon passes for a dainty ; and so does braised beef garnished with pickled cherries or apples. One must see a Frenchman munching a pickled apple to understand what consternation is. By and by a salad is brought in— potatoes, chicory, dandelion, and radishes mixed up with anchovies, vinegar, and brown sugar. Here the polite Frenchman's brow breaks out into moisture ; but he revives at the sight of a sponge cake steeped in rum, which has at least the merit of being so pungent as to take away the taste of all the previous courses. As soon as the cloth is removed cigarettes are brought in with tea and lemons, instead of cream, and the Russian host begins to puff away until what with the fumes of tobacco, the heat of the stove, and the indigestion which the dinner has produced, the guest's head begins to turn. Then the host says compassionately, 'Try a little vodki.'

CHAPTER XXXIV.

DIPLOMATISTS.

RUSSIAN diplomatists have long enjoyed the reputation which Epimenides gave to the Cretans—Κρῆτες ἀεὶ ψεῦσται; but it must be considered that if they had not so constantly practised Telleyrand's maxim about speech being given to man for the purpose of disguising thought, their country would never have thriven as it has.

Russia has gone on expanding and encroaching by blinding and deceiving other nations; and we say nations advisedly, for it is only the masses who have been deceived, not the statesmen, who have never rated Russian good faith above its value. But if a statesman having suspicions cannot get his countrymen to share them, his perspicacity serves little; so it has been the aim of Russian diplomatists to mislead peoples rather than the men who ruled them.

If they could hoax a statesman, so much the better—they bagged him, so to say, and made him comfortable; but in constitutional countries their object has always been the Parliament ; and in States where the popular voice counts for little, the Court.

Russian diplomatists are always clever men who have served an apprenticeship in their craft by plotting in those boudoir cabals which in St. Petersburg are the mainsprings of home politics. No dullard could carry off an important post amid the fierce competitions which these cabals excite ; and this may lead us to remark, by the way, that there is no system of government which brings talent to the front so well as a thorough-paced despotism.

When a Russian secures an ambassadorship, it does not mean merely that he is in the good books of Prince Gortschakoff; it signifies that he has a strong official party at his back, and leaves behind him a number of persons, including ladies, who will sing his praises under all circumstances. If he falls it is because his cabal has ceased to be powerful ; but so long as he holds his post he enjoys an independence of action unknown to the diplomatists of other countries.

And he possesses two other points of superiority : first, his unlimited command of secret-service money ; and, secondly, his total irresponsibility as regards public opinion in his own country. The lie that would damn an English plenipotentiary if clearly brought home to him is accounted no disgrace to a Russian in his own land. Ninety-nine-hundredths of the people never hear of it, and the few who do are the polite classes, who hold that fibbing is a part of the science of life. As for the foreigners to whom the untruth has been told, they may console themselves by reflecting that they had never believed it, or if they had let themselves be duped, they deem it prudent not to murmur, feeling, 'honteux comme un renard qu'une poule aurait pris.'

The importance of the different embassies varies according to circumstances, and one capital may sometimes require an astuter man than another; but Russia seldom changes her envoys from post to post, each Ambassador being accounted specially fitted for the country to which he is accredited.

Baron Brunnow, who so long filled the embassy in London, would not have shone in Paris, where his ponderous placidity and smileless hauteur would have passed for arrogance. He was a genial man after the English fashion, and was seen at his best when talking to some Tory nobleman about agriculture and sports which he understood and loved. He spoke English faultlessly, and liked English books, customs, and dinners. He could make an after-dinner speech, pick out a good horse among the Derby favourites and back

him ; and few appraised so shrewdly as he the merits
of the rising men in Parliament.

But he twice made a capital mistake in discrimi-
nation—the first time when he thought the days of
England's warring had entirely ceased, which mistake
led to the Crimean War ; the second mistake, which
pervaded all his conduct to the time of his retirement,
was to think that by continually fomenting British
jealousies as to French ambition he could draw England and Russia along with Austria into a concert for
the partition of the Turkish Empire. Baron Brunnow's hobby was a Tory England allied to Russia
against France, which was his bugbear.

His successor, Count Schouvaloff, is a man of
fewer illusions, and endowed with much less sympathy with things English, though he, too, has
manners which Englishmen like. A former general
of cavalry, who afterwards filled the office of Minister
of Police, he has that quiet urbanity which nothing
can ruffle and that patience in listening (seeming
to agree with the speaker all the while) which is a
great art.

Painfully polite with small folk, from whom he
has nothing to hope ; cheery when it is his business
to look pleasant, and earnestly persuasive when he
has 'assurances' to give, he is perhaps of all diplo-

matists the best fashioned for 'talking over' politicians
of shallow wit.   Now and then the bluntness of the
cavalry officer breaks out in his utterances and he
strokes his thick moustache with a scowl.   But he
masters himself in a moment.   It must be a very stupid,
shuffling minister who provokes him to grimace in
this way ; and he seems to reflect on second thoughts
that it is not worth his while to be angry with the
creature.   Count Schouvaloff has a peculiar mordant
wit which he uses upon occasions ; and his contempt
for popular institutions, journalists, and Liberal politicians is so complete that it verges upon indulgence.
Think of what must be felt towards Liberals by a
former Minister of Police—a man who has transported more of these gentlemen to Siberia than would
fill Westminster Hall and Trafalgar Square too !

A very different person is Prince Orloff, the Ambassador to Paris, who is French to his finger-tips, and
uses no flattery when he tells Frenchmen that theirs
is the country of the globe which he most esteems.   A
simpering, emotional statesman, who shed tears publicly
at M. Thiers's funeral ; a lover of art, who crowds his
drawing-rooms with artists and authors ; a sceptic,
who assiduously attends the debates at Versailles and
looks as if he keenly enjoyed himself every time he
sees the Republicans play a bout against the Church,

monarchism, or militaryism—Prince Orloff has made more friends for himself than for his country.

As a diplomatist, indeed, he has been a failure, for all his attempts to allay French suspiciousness of Russian aggression have failed. Even M. Thiers, whom the Prince used affectionately to call 'cher maître,' remembered very well how Russia had abetted Germany in 1870; and he was aware that in present times the voice of the Prince d'Oubril is more potent in Russian councils than those of the Orloff family. Moreover, it is Princess Lise Trou-betzkoi who is the real Ambassador to Paris. This small, dainty lady, with the sharp grey eyes and chirping laugh, is more trusted than Prince Orloff. It is she who holds Gortschakoff's *carte-blanche* to make terms with French statesmen, and who for some time past has been trying her blandishments on the 'coming man' of France—M. Gambetta. But M. Gambetta will not be caught.

Prince d'Oubril is the Russian Ambassador to Berlin—a diplomatist who looks cut out of a book of military tailoring patterns, so very stiff and Prussian is he. He and his first secretary, Count E. von Kotze-bue, are the two chief links in the family alliance between the Romanoffs and Hohenzollerns.

Their mission seems to be to persuade the Emperor

William that the Russian Court is infatuated about everything German.

Prince d'Oubril never misses a review or a military levée. Holding an honorary lieutenant-colonelcy in some Prussian regiment, he wears its uniform in preference to his own. He speaks German to his attachés and servants; he gives dinners on all the Prussian patriotic anniversaries, and clothes his residence with bunting on all the kaiserliche-königliche birthdays. He devours beer-soup and potatoes stewed with prunes to prove that his palate as well as his heart is German.

Whether Prince Bismarck likes this so Prussian Russian it is difficult to say; but, anyhow, Prince d'Oubril exercises his influence through other channels than the Chancellor's; he is less of an ambassador than a confidant, who acts as intermediary for the relations of two reigning houses whose friendship is independent of political considerations. He dines with Kaiser Wilhelm on days when no other diplomatists are invited; and at Court parties he may be seen conversing with his Majesty for half-hours at a time.

His authority is so well established that it overshadows that of Count Novikoff, who is ambassador to Vienna, and has had for several years past a most difficult part to play. The Hapsburgs used once to

be even greater allies of the Russian Imperial family
than the Hohenzollerns, but the Crimean War upset
the good understanding ; and now, since the Sadowa
campaign, the Emperor Francis Joseph has been fain
to perceive that every friendly demonstration from
Alexander to William and *vice versâ* can bode no
good to himself.

M. Novikoff, who is known to be a Prussophobian,
or who at least affects so to be, has doubtless spent
a good deal of his time in explaining privately to
Count Andrassy that the Russo-Prussian alliance is
only a make-believe, and that Alexander II. would
gladly recall the days when Francis Joseph's bust in
marble was the sole ornament of Nicholas's study. But
whether he will succeed in converting a Hungarian
nobleman who saw his country invaded by Russian
troops in 1848, and who was himself sentenced to be
hanged as a rebel in that year, remains to be seen.

The drawback to Russian diplomacy is that all
its exponents seem to be pulling different ways, so
that if a statesman be inclined to credit what one
Ambassador says, he soon learns that another in a
neighbouring Court is insinuating just the contrary,
and swearing to it too. Even so must the Cretans
have transacted business in the days when they had
ambassadors.

CHAPTER XXXV.

THE FUTURE OF TO-DAY.

IF anybody had inquired two years ago as to the future of Russia, the answer he would have received would have been very different from the one that would be vouchsafed to him now. Russia seemed then to be hurrying towards her fall.

Embroiled in financial difficulties, distracted by intestine plots, plagued with an administrative corruption so deep that its effects were felt under the form of a festering discontent in all classes, it was evident that a fierce crisis was approaching, and that the first phase of it would be war.

Corrupt States in difficulties always think of war; and Russia had one of those big, ill-paid, ill-officered armies which if not turned to account for the purpose of slaughtering foreigners are apt to become mutinous at home.

The danger was so pressing that the Czar became hypochondriacal. This was perceived by all who came near him. The melancholy madness that had run through the veins of Paul, of Alexander, of Nicholas in the last months of his life seemed to have marked out a new victim in the Prince who had begun his reign with noble acts, but who had been turned from his natural bent of graciousness by the influences of a dissolute Court and by evil counsellors.

Evidently the Czar feared war scarcely less than peace; but there lay the implacable alternative between some savage revolution in which the Throne would be overturned or a war in which, by hook or by crook, some glory might be won to consolidate his throne for a little while longer—and so he chose war; or rather his advisers chose it for him. But in his heart he had little hope of success; and certainly those who watched his reckless adventure had at first still less.

There was not a politician in Europe but knew that the grievances of the oppressed Christians in Turkey, which the most bloody-handed Government in the world took for its war-cry, were but a paltry pretence; and it was considered certain that England, whose interests were menaced by a Russian war of aggression, would interfere, amid the approval, if not with the alliance, of every free State in Christendom.

Had England done this, Turkey, saved from destruction by British arms, must have yielded to British advice as to the government of her subject provinces, which would then have got better terms than they are ever likely to obtain from Russia; and the latter country, overthrown as a dominant military Power, would before long have found regeneration as a free community.

It may be said that a European war might have resulted from British interference in the East. Perhaps; but with England, France, Austria, Italy, Denmark, Holland, and Belgium all on one side, the outcome of a general war would have been the satisfactory settlement of all the questions pending between State and State. Europe would have entered into a long and strengthening peace like that which followed Waterloo; and certainly if there was a class of men who, more than another, had a solid interest in seeing this state of things come to pass, that class ought to have included the Liberals in every country.

But it was precisely the British Liberals who caused matters to take a different turn. Led on by the statesman who had formerly denounced the despotic rule of King Bomba in Naples, these men, blinded by party passion, and amid the astonishment of the Liberals in every other country, raised the cry

of Russian humanity and disinterestedness, forsooth !
They gave Russia a strength which her arms would
never have secured for her.   They sealed the fate of
Turkey, threw their Bulgarian *protégés* under the
Russian heel, and sowed 'the seeds of many a future
war.   It would have taken a clearsighted Liberal to
predict that a party of peace and progress would
ever act in this way, at the bidding of a man soured
at having lost his popularity and burning to revenge
himself by hampering his successor in office.

But the mischief has been done, and it behoves
one less to mourn over what is irrevocable than to
examine the probable results of the most stupendous
piece of political waywardness that ever placed a great
country in jeopardy.

First, the progress of Russia in civilization has
been indefinitely adjourned ; for the condition of popular sentiment in the country is such that the Government cannot concede one reform without yielding
many ; and, as these reforms would involve the
sweeping away of the Tschinn, the tschinovniks who
hold the power in their hands will prefer to yield
nothing.   Why should they do so when, now that
the nation is elated by victory, they can keep it under
control by turning its thoughts towards new and
greater conquests in the future ?

A people that is being trained in the arts of war for some specific purpose forgets its burdens and grievances. Present discomforts are lightened by prospect of a better time coming, when there will be spoils to share and honours to show; and if some reflect that there cannot be spoils and honours for everybody, whereas all may count upon a share of hardships and wounds, these are the few whose voices are not heard amid the general martial clamour.

Russian peacemongers are going to have a poor time of it; for a greater war than Russia ever waged before is held to be preparing, and this time the enemy will be England. There will be no concealment about it. All over that vast country, which covers an extent half as large as Europe, it is known already that Russia has given England a buffet, and to-morrow it will be known that England, fretful under her humiliation, has become a menace for Russian interests.

With such fables as ignorant, half-barbarous peoples easily swallow, it will be told to the hungry mujick that England is the country which prevents him from bettering himself at the expense of the sunny kingdoms of Hindustan. Where these kingdoms lie the mujick does not know; but he will dream of them, and be ready to fight for them when the time comes.

Meanwhile, there will be no stinting of Russian armaments—no questioning as to whether six millions, or sixteen, or sixty can be afforded for the work of making Russia fit to satiate her ambition. The money will be found somewhere by loans and heaped-up taxes ; and every year gold will be squandered in piles to provide artillery, improved rifles, and gaudily-equipped regiments, for a country which has scarcely any schools, pavements, or drains.

To keep pace with so gigantic an armament, England will have to put forth her best too, or else she will lose India. It is of no use to blink this issue. There will be no need to invade India : a new mutiny would serve Russia's purpose quite as well, and better. From the moment when Turkey was struck down England had no ally in the East, and, what is worse, Turkish influence under Russian direction will stir up the fanaticism of forty millions of Indian Mussulmans against us.

England's possessions must now be guarded by herself alone, and it will be the better for her if she at once accepts the fact that she cannot guard them with such forces as have hitherto sufficed. Liberal policy has laid upon her the necessity of soon quadrupling her army and doubling her fleet; and the best that an Englishman can hope is that his countrymen will proceed to do this while it is yet time, and not wait till a disaster lights upon them.

Ultimately, of course, Russia must be overtaken by the fate that comes upon all barbarous States that grow too big. It must fall to pieces.

The old Muscovites, who foresee this, have never been anxious for the conquest of Constantinople, knowing that this city would shortly become the capital of the Empire; and that between the races established in indolent ease among the provinces of the sunny south and those hardened in the cold climate of the north there would be a disruption.

Neither can Russia eternally stave off the difficulties engendered by the Socialism that lurks in country districts and the fanatical Nihilism which is smouldering in the towns. The day will come when the sword must be sheathed, and when home questions will struggle to the front; and then the dangers of a mighty convulsion that will heave up the whole country and plunge it into anarchy will arise.

But this is looking far afield; and it is enough for England that when Plevna fell Russia renewed her lease of military power and turbulence for another

generation at least. She has become an overt enem
whom Englishmen cannot afford to ignore—least ‹
all to despise. England can still prevent her froɪ
doing her worst ; but it is only vigilance and strengt
that will check her, not sentiment and weakness.

And we are bound to remember that in stayin
Russian aggression we shall be discharging a sacre,
duty, incumbent on us as Christians and true Liberal
We have taken upon ourselves to reclaim a hundre
and fifty millions of Indians from a barbarism int
which they would soon relapse if our guiding hand
failed them. It is a holy task, from which we muɪ
not suffer ourselves to be diverted. Posterity wi
hold us accountable for it, and God's blessing will nc
fail us in prosecuting it now, if we are steadfast, as w
ought to be, in so good a cause.

LONDON : PRINTED BY
SPOTTISWOODE AND CO., NEW-STREET SQUARE
AND PARLIAMENT STREET

www.ingramcontent.com/pod-product-compliance
Lightning Source LLC
Chambersburg PA
CBHW021212270326
41929CB00010B/1096